Jack

By

Anne Booth

To Joan & Ray
Best wishes
Jack W th

All royalties from this book will be donated to Cancer Research

Jack

At the age of 90 and encouraged by members of his family, Jack Wilson decided to write his memoirs – no mean task for someone of his age to undertake. His life has been to say the least, eventful, and no-one can say that he hasn't lived life to the full. In his ninety-first year, he is still full of life, enjoying his garden and meetings with his friends at the Probus club, but I think I can say with certainty that most of all, he enjoys spending time with his ever growing family.

With three children, six grandchildren and eleven great grandchildren, he never needs to be short of company and his wallet is always open! Jack has experienced poverty as a child, the horrors of war, excitement and danger as a policeman and the joys that a family can bring. He has old fashioned values and principles and isn't afraid to let you know if you cross these boundaries; but can be gentle and caring, showing great affection to those he loves. He is careful with his hard earned money whilst being generous and giving. Jack is also a proud man; proud of his own achievements and those of his family, letting everyone know of each new accomplishment or success made by his loved ones. Well known to many, a trip to the local library will often result in conversations with old friends and acquaintances and it is inspiring to see just how well liked he is. Although my name is on the front of this book as the author, it is mainly written in the first person as Jack wrote down his notes. He has spent many hours writing, no mean fcat for a ninety year old man. I have simply been the caretaker of this work, but it has been a great pleasure and the time taken to complete this project has kept us both busy! As a father, father-in-law, grandfather and great grandfather, he has witnessed the highs and lows of family life, taking pleasure and pride in the good times, and experiencing the sadness and disappointments of the sad times. Most of all, he is a normal family man. He is Jack Wilson…

… Anne Booth Wilson

Early Days

In a pictorial book entitled 'Old Clitheroe', there is a photo with the caption: 'A photograph of West View when it really was West View'. Although the family lived at 11 West View, my mother actually gave birth to me at my grandma's house in 28 Woone Lane on the 4th of November 1923. My father John and mother Elizabeth had met when they were weavers at Whipp Cotton Mill. Elizabeth Clark operated six looms and John Wilson ran four looms. Dad was a Methodist and mother went to St James Church of England which is where they were married. I was born two years after their marriage, and it is only now when I have written Nan's story, do I know that the family doctor, Cooper, had married a daughter of the Garnett family who years after my birth employed Nan, my future wife.

Number 11 West View had three rooms upstairs and three rooms downstairs. There was no bathroom and we had gas for lighting and the oven. There was no electricity as we were never able to afford to have it. Each room had a gas light and only in the living room was there a fitting which held three mantles. There were two thin chains coming from the fitting in the ceiling. One chain switched the gas on and the other switched it off. Coming into the house when it was pitch black meant you had to be prepared. We came into the corridor from the outside door, opened the sitting room door with a match ready, pulled the light chain and as the gas flowed, we lit the mantle. The mantles were very fragile and so if you touched the mantle with the wood of the match, the mantle would break. Jim Buller's shop came in very handy then as he sold the replacement mantles. If the fire was already burning, then a taper lit from the fire was easier than a match. The gas meter only held pennies and on odd occasions, we didn't have any. A gas man came once a month and counted out what was in the meter. He used to

2

stack them in piles of twelve which made exactly a shilling, and depending how much we had spent, he would decide on how much we got back in rebate.

There was no such thing as fitted carpets. We had oil cloth all over the floors and no money for anything else. The front downstairs room and one of the two back bedrooms were never used, so there was no furniture in them. My bedroom consisted of a single bed which I had to share with my brother Cecil when he arrived ten years later. The coal fire with an oven at the side was the central point of the house and we did have a rug in front of the fire which made it a bit cosier. It had been made by my mother using old clothes which were cut into small pieces and pegged into a piece of hessian and commonly known as a peg rug. The furniture consisted of a dresser, a wooden table, a sofa, a rocking chair and three wooden chairs. Years later we possessed an old radio, which more often than not hardly ever worked.

The back garden was 15 yards in length and next to the back yard gate was the toilet. They were tippler toilets and I won't try and describe it but every so often, the thing below you made a funny noise, tipped upside down and the contents would then flow into the sewers. Toilet rolls were never contemplated; it was squares of newspaper on a string attached to the toilet door. Woone Lane, Wilson St and Mitchell St were all on the modern toilet systems. We had a small greenhouse, an aviary for budgerigars, a small pen for bantams, a square yard bed of mint which brought in quite a number of pennies per bunch as no-one near us had any; and there was a dog kennel for Rover who was a lovely mongrel which was part Labrador and part Airedale. After a few years, Rover was run over by a car and died. There were three feet high brick walls between all the gardens which rose to six feet when opposite the kitchens of each property. People used to discuss all sorts of topics over these garden walls.

Next door at number 9 was the Braithwaite family and they had a son Brian aged 10 and a girl Betty who was 3 months older than me. Mr Braithwaite was a joiner and this was his second marriage, his first wife having died aboard the Titanic. Apparently, the moment we were able to walk, Betty and I were like brother and sister and we were in and out of each other's homes, becoming childhood friends until the age of thirteen. Mr Braithwaite was the top maintenance man at a mental hospital so his wife never worked. There was therefore a large difference in income between the two families, but it made no difference to that beautiful little curly haired girl and I.

In the booklet 'Old Clitheroe', there were no houses opposite, but in 1923, there was a row of houses there and a shop across from us. Bullers sold everything you could imagine, groceries, medicines, clothing, confectionary, sweets; a remarkable little corner shop. Jim Buller was a St John's Ambulance man which came in handy. I can remember 'All Fours' cough mixture as being the favoured medicine.

Many business people lived in West View, including several school teachers. The bottom house was detached and owned by a doctor; its garden and garage covering the space of numbers 1, 3, 5 and 7 in the street. There were four streets running parallel to one another; Woone Lane, Wilson St, West View and Mitchell St, and Nan and I later had number 1 Mitchell St as our first home. My Clarke grandparents lived in Woone Lane, my Aunt Connie and Uncle Tom lived in Wilson St which was later owned by my parents, and we lived in West View. They all had cobbled back streets which were all interlinked and so I was able to go to each home via the back gardens. Woone Lane was a shopping street with the Co-op, two fish and chip shops, a newsagent, a hardware shop, a butcher, a men's outfitters, a hairdresser, two sweet shops, another grocers, an ice-cream shop, a greengrocer, a bike shop, a builder's yard and a confectioners. One of the fish and chip shops was opposite grandma's house and I remember wondering whether or not I would ever be able to see above the counter. Grandma's house was also used as a

4

milk shop for Uncle Tom's business selling milk at 3d a pint. There were little shops in almost every street in the town. Clitheroe Castle was very close, just north of our streets and the castle field where I seemed to spend most of my time was only 100 yards away.

When I was five years old, mother and father were still working at Whipp Mill and they had a half hour break for their breakfast. All mill workers wore clogs and there was a right clatter when they came back to get me ready for school. I don't think anyone locked their doors in those days, and I didn't see them again after that until after 5:30pm. I think that they worked from 7am until 5:30 pm, perhaps longer. I went off to school in my clogs usually with Betty from next door, but she wore shoes. We stayed in the same class together until the age of 11, always in the top six or seven pupils.

As a young woman, Betty joined the W.A.A.F's and I only saw her once in her uniform and she looked very smart and pretty. Later she married a Clitheroe man and they went to live in Africa where she had two children. Her brother Brian remained single, living in 9 West View and he became the Clitheroe Registrar. Betty and her husband were well off and had a large house in Africa with servants. However, with all the unrest and fighting there, they returned to live in the South of England, near Bournemouth. Whenever she visited her brother, she always went to see my mother. In about 1990, I was visiting my mother when she told me that Betty had just been to see her so I went round to 9 West View straight away and Betty recognised me immediately. However, if I had not known that it was Betty, I would not have recognised her as the little girl of so long ago. She was very thin, haggard and looked twenty years older than I. Betty kissed me and we spent a short time talking about what had happened to the two of us since we had last met. I never saw her again.

If I wanted anything to eat at lunchtime, it would only take two minutes to go to Grandma Clarke's, but often I didn't bother and stayed in St James school yard to play football. None of the old junior schools had a grass playing field. The front yard of the school was the girls' playing area and the back was for the lads. It was approximately fifty yards square and made of tarmacadam, being slightly sloped towards the bottom boundary wall which separated the school yard from a slow moving stream, Mearley Brook. Throughout the whole of my Primary school years this was our football pitch. Imagine… a hundred and fifty lads kicking a soft ball, all wearing clogs with irons on the bottom. Very few under seven joined in but I was in from my first day at the age of five. The ball often went over the wall and into the brook, but it was the older lads who had to retrieve it. In frosty weather the yard was like an ice rink and there were three slides in operation. We could go at a fair lick down these slides with our iron shod clogs before we finished up against the bottom wall. These days, our schools would probably have some concerns regarding 'health and safety' for the children sliding dangerously along these icy strips. At the age of nine, I asked the headmaster Mr Gregson, if I could form a school football team to play the other two large infant schools, Pendle Juniors and the Roman Catholics. He agreed and I became the very first school captain. We played on the Castle field football pitch and the other two schools had their own grass pitches.

At school, I was always very good at maths, geography and drawing, but useless at painting and English language. Many years later I found out that I was colour blind and so it was no wonder that I wasn't very good at painting. I was also good at history and spelling. The time I spent at St James' was lovely and time passed so quickly. I still remember all the teachers' names; one male and five female; four of whom were unmarried and the male teacher must have had a whale of a time.

The back, cobbled street between West View and Wilson St was a wonderful pitch, 100 yards long. Goal posts weren't needed as the two ends of the street sufficed.

When the ball lofted over the back gardens, it was recovered by opening the nearest unlocked garden gate and then climbing over the internal garden walls to retrieve the ball. We often played twenty a side with sometimes dads playing as well. Money was always tight and every penny counted as it probably did for all the other mill working families.

The back street was also a cricket pitch, wonderful for concentration as the ball hit the cobbles. The wicket was chalked onto the doctor's garage door and rubbed off at the end of the match. Monday was always washing day, and as washing was strung across the backs from the hooks outside each house, it was never possible to play then. Rag and bone men used the backs as did the horse drawn coal carts, and there was always lots of horse manure to shovel up to use for the gardens. There was no need for artificial manure then. Milk men however used the front streets.

My Wilson grandparents had died before I was born and their grave is in Clitheroe Cemetery. Sarah was their eldest child and she married Harry Robinson. They had one son, William who at the age of eighteen joined the Welsh Regiment and went off to fight in the First World War in 1917. He was killed on 17th April 1918, a month before his nineteenth birthday, by a shell in the Battle of the Somme and his body was never found. The Clitheroe Advertiser at the time, revealed that Tom Seedall, one of Willie's friends, had contacted Sarah and Harry after their son's death and was able to explain to them how he had died.

The following is taken from that article which was published about the 10th May: ' *On Friday afternoon last, Mr and Mrs Harry Robinson, Moss St, were overwhelmed with grief on learning of the death of their son, William, who crossed to France with other 'eighteeners' on Easter Monday. The sad news was forwarded by a pal, Tom Seedall, who, writing the previous Sunday stated that Private Robinson had been killed instantaneously by the*

7

bursting of a shell in the trench'.....

In Tom's letter he told Willie's devastated parents: '*It grieves me to tell you about your son Willie, but I think it my duty to write to you as Willie and I have been the best of pals ever since we met at Kinmell Park last June, and we had been together ever since, even up to his death. We were in the trench when a shell dropped quite close, and Willie was killed outright. We all feel his loss very much; it nearly broke my heart when I saw him killed. He was ever cheerful, even when we were in the trenches and always a good lad.'*

The Advertiser also revealed something about William that I had never known. Written in the last sentence was the little snippet of information stating that he had been the youngest bell-ringer at the Parish Church where they held him in high esteem.

Memorial tributes of sympathy were sent to the newspaper, two of which are very poignant. William's parents wrote:

'Oh for the sound of the voice we loved,
The smile on those lips now sealed.
Oh, for the touch of a vanished hand,
The wound in our hearts to heal
We pictured his safe returning.
We longed to clasp his hand.
But God has postponed the meeting
Till we meet in the Better land.

Another, from Ethel the girl he had left behind...

The face we loved is now laid low,
His fond, true heart is still.
The hand we clasped when we said good-bye,
Lies low in death's cold chill.
He nobly answered duties call,
He gave his life for one and all;
But the unknown grave is the bitterest blow

None but an aching heart can know.

His memorial is at Passchendaele in Belgium. Sarah and her husband were never able to recover from his death and his photo along with his war medals were displayed on the wall in their home for all to see until they died. From the day I was born, I received the love and attention from Aunt Sarah and Uncle Harry that they had been unable to give their son after he had died. William's favourite book was the 1909 edition of 'Chatterbox' and as soon as I was able to take care of things, it was given to me. I treasured it immediately. In 1964 when I went to live in Heywood as Police Inspector, I purchased a new garden shed and until we could get organised I put several cardboard boxes containing different items in it; one of which contained books. The shed door was frequently open during the daytime and on one occasion I saw wood-mice near the shed and inside the shed a carton had a large hole in the side. The mice had made their nest inside the box and young mice were running in all directions. It was of course the carton of books and as I examined each book, I was dismayed to find that each one was damaged. I took out the 'Chatterbox' with baited breath and was very relieved to find that unlike the majority of the other books, this one was in one piece. I have distributed Sunday school prizes at Heywood Baptist Chapel and also at St Luke's Church, and I have told the children about William Robinson, who each year of his boyhood received a Sunday school prize for good attendance and about how he died fighting for his country. I also related the story of the charmed life of his favourite book which I would carefully hold in my hands and show them. It is about forty years since I last told the story of the 'Chatterbox' in the Baptist Chapel, but the children, now of course adults, still remember.

Uncle James was my Wilson grandparent's second child and he ran Chatburn Nursery gardens. James married Janie and they too only had one child, Winifred, who married Fred Broome. Winifred and Fred had a son called

Raymond but Winifred died quite early, before I was born, and so Uncle James and Aunt Janey adopted Raymond their grandson. Uncle Arthur was the third child of my Wilson grandparents and he owned a bakery in the Belle View area of Manchester. He did have children, but we didn't see Uncle Arthur and his family very often. My father John was the youngest of the children born to my Wilson grandparents.

My other grandfather James Clarke married Frances Bowker. It was his second marriage as his first wife had died. He worked at Barrow Print Works and my grandma never worked. The first of their children was Elizabeth, my mother; then Rachel who remained a spinster all her life. Thomas followed and he married Constance Minshull who coincidentally was the illegitimate daughter of Arthur Wilson, but Thomas and Connie were never able to have children. This meant that I was the only child of the Clarke family until my brother Cecil was born ten years later.

At this point in my story, between the ages of four and seven, there are so many things that I recall, but putting them in any sort of order is more difficult. The local football league played on Saturday mornings; being mostly church teams and my dad played for the Wesleyan Chapel. Sometimes on Saturday afternoons, he would take me to watch Blackburn Rovers play, either by bus or train and he would plonk me over the low wall alongside the pitch where I would sit next to the hundreds of little lads all around the ground. At other times on Saturday afternoons, Grandma Clarke, Aunt Rachel and mother would take me to Blackburn market by bus and tram or train and they would always buy shrimps and oysters. I often got a 1d book and outside the train station in Blackburn were folk selling hot potatoes, so I always got a bag of those too.

Mother and Aunt Rachel were Sunday school teachers, so each Sunday not only did I attend the morning and afternoon church services, but also went to Sunday school twice a day as well. Grandma paid pew rent and we were in the second pew from the front so I had to be quiet and respectful, especially to the vicar's wife who sat in the opposite pew. On Tuesday evenings, I went to the 'Band of Hope'.

I was one of the two page boys when the annual Cotton Queen was held and Whipp Mill won it. When mother took her Sunday school girls on picnics, I went with them and I was always exhausted because sometimes they walked ten miles or more. Aunt Sarah and Uncle Harry were also fond of walking and we would go up hills and down dales throughout the Ribble valley, so I was a pretty fit individual. Uncle Harry was the engineer at Clitheroe Gas Works and when he retired, it took six different men to replace him. He also used to take me to the Gas Works on Saturday mornings to inspect everything that moved. We would climb up the outside steps to the top of the large gas holder; then inside the holder was a metal folding ladder which we descended. I was able to ride on the works railway engine which shunted coal waggons around. It was very exciting and no thought was given to danger, but I was in good hands. We went back to his house for Saturday lunch which was always sausages and mash; then I got three pennies spending money.

I had never ridden a bike until at the age of seven, Uncle Tom who had a milk round, decided to teach me on Aunt Connie's bike. There were very few cars ever used on Wilson Street and so it was safe. It took me a day or two to get used to it, and then he said that I could go a little bit further. I rode into West View then Mitchell Street. At the bottom of Mitchell Street was a large double gate which was open and led into the Castle grounds. In through the gate I went, then along the path which divided left and right around a flower bed. There was a small two foot high wire mesh shielding the plants. It was decision time; left or right, but I hadn't time to go either way. The front wheel hit the mesh and I nose- dived over the front of the bike and flattened about fifteen very large dahlia plants in full bloom. That was the end of my cycling days until I got my own bike at the age of ten.

Grandad had retired at about this time so my grandparents were struggling along; but nevertheless, they seemed to manage. Christmas Day was always a wonderful time. Father Christmas came and got a cup of coffee and a piece of cake. One year I got a rocking horse. Father Christmas was always grandad, but of course I never knew that. One way I made a bit of money was to be the 'first-footer' on New Year's Eve. With having black hair, I had to be the first one into a number of homes to bring in the New Year. One of these homes was that of a school teacher and Aunt Sarah's house was a must.

Throughout my early years, Dad was steward at the Methodist Church billiards room. There were two tables and also a table tennis room and a reading room. He went every weekday evening and was responsible for the upkeep of the tables as well as taking the payments from members. I often went with him and if no-one was using the table tennis tables, he would play with me. I became quite good and it wasn't long before the members realised that I could give them a good game and so let me play. Eventually I could beat them all and at the age of thirteen I became Junior Champion in both singles and doubles in the Ribble Valley League.

During the 1930's there was a cotton crisis and entire factories were closing throughout the North West. Both mother and father were without jobs. Six mills closed in Clitheroe leaving only two to survive, one of which was Holmes Mill opposite St James' school. Mother and father walked the ten miles to Blackburn to find work, but after a few months they got work again at Holmes Mill, although their wages were far short of the wages they had previously earned. Soon, Holmes Mill closed and it was the end of Clitheroe as a cotton town. It was a difficult time for my parents and in spite of all their efforts nothing came of their walking from town to town in search of work. They queued up at the employment exchange for hours with all the other hundreds of people and also had to queue for the small amount of dole money that they

12

received.

At one time dad bought himself an extension ladder, found some customers and cleaned windows. One icy day he fell off the ladder and that was the end of the window cleaning. Mother also found a few people who needed a cleaner and so she cleaned their homes. Once a year at the annual mayor-making ceremony, the Mayor, Councillors and leaders in the town had a reception in the Swan and Royal Hotel, and the following day the Swan and Royal dished out soup to the poor children in the town. Each child would take a jug and hundreds queued pitifully in the pub yard. When the front of the queue was reached, the jug was filled with soup and an apple and orange also given. I was in that queue. Once I had returned home the soup was warmed up and it became the meal for the whole family.

In the autumn when the mushrooms were growing in the country fields, my father and I set off at five am to pick them. Dad knew the best fields at Greenbridge and Edisford and if we were lucky enough to be the first there, we would collect them in a large handkerchief. It provided two meals for that day; firstly fried on toast, and later the stems and peelings were boiled in milk.

During the time when both of my parents were working there was one week's holiday a year which was wakes week and at that time a week's train ticket for an adult to go on day trips cost ten shillings. Popular destinations were Barrow-In-Furness, Windermere, Morecambe, Blackpool, Southport, New Brighton, Llandudno and anywhere in between. We were able to go on these trips. One day when I was four years old we were in Blackpool Zoo, which at that time was in the Tower buildings. There were very large animals in the cages including lions and tigers. Suddenly there was panic with hundreds of people dashing for the outer doors shouting 'Lion loose!' Mother grabbed me and held on tightly. It was a hoax by pick pockets, creating a crush of people and stealing from their pockets wallets and watches.

From the age of five until fourteen I went on holiday

13

every year for a week with Grandma and Aunt Rachel. Grandad didn't go with us. We always went to Llandudno Junction and we stayed with a family called Parry. Mr Parry was a railway engine driver and they had a son called Gwilliam who was my age. They were wonderful times; the weather always seemed to be warm and we went up Great Orme on the cable railway, to Aber Falls, on coach trips and boat trips on the River Conwy, and visited castles. When we got back to the house, there was always Gwilliam to play with. Mother and dad always came to Llandudno to see us when it was a cheap trip on the Wednesday, but I always felt sad when we waved them off at the station as they set off back home. It just didn't seem right for them to get just one day's holiday.

Dad made a two wheeled hand truck which we used for collecting bags of coal from the railway sidings as it was cheaper than getting it from the coal man. If I wasn't with my grandparents on holiday, I used to cover the inside of the truck with a cloth and wait at the castle gate for the holiday makers. It was a mile to the station and I carted their luggage bags and usually received 6d for each journey. The trains were running every half an hour, so when I reached the station I ran quickly back to catch the next trippers.

We always had a bonfire outside our back door, and there used to be another one further up the cobbled back street. One day, whilst we little lads were playing football in the backs, there appeared a crowd of folk encircling two men stripped to the waist. Neighbours from the houses at the top end of the street were watching and a right royal fist fight ensued between a hulking teenager and a thin wiry chap twice his age, but half his size. I don't know who won, but later on when I became a policeman I recognised the little chap who by now was the road engine driver in the Highways Dept.

In 1933 Cecil was born, leaving a gap of ten years between the two of us; but I later discovered that mother had suffered two early miscarriages in between. Dad

14

finally found a new job as the Dairyman at the Coop at Chaigley which was five miles from Clitheroe. He went to work on a bike and he retained that job until he became very ill with cancer and in 1950 died at the age of sixty two.

At the age of ten, I have a vague recollection of sitting for the Grammar School exam and failing it. My childhood dream was to become an engine driver, but that was no excuse for failing the exam. I had not done my homework and it would undoubtedly have been the English paper which let me down. I was not dismayed as even as a child I realised that there would have been a problem for mother buying the uniform and all the other requirements for the Grammar School. Betty of course passed as did three of my best friends. One of them, Arthur Pollard, had a remarkable memory and never revised. He became head boy of Clitheroe Royal Grammar School, went to Hull University, became a Don and ended his career at Canterbury Cathedral. I remained friends with the Grammar School brigade until we finally went our separate ways.

I mention for the first time a friend of my age who went with me to the Day School, Sunday school, Church choir and football. He was called Walter Clayton and his parents were good friends of my parents. I will return to him later.

Between the ages of eight and ten, my parents never knew where I was apart from the fact that I would be with my mates. We spent a lot of time in the castle grounds, playing on the cannon from the First World War. There was also a tank from the war in Brungerley Park where we spent many hours messing inside the tank with all the levers. We made fires in the old quarry at Crosshills near the cement works and also played in the pond. Of course, the River Ribble; especially by Edisford Bridge, was an exciting place to play and we spent many hours fishing for bull heads, trout, minnows and whiskers. We fished at Greenbridge where there were sticklebacks, minnows and kingfishers. It certainly was a life spent in the countryside.

15

The parents of one of our pals owned a farm where we also played. We would bring back lots of wild flowers such as dog daisies, primroses, primulas, bluebells, hairbells, orchids, mayflowers and violets. We collected Iris and bulrushes from the ponds as well as chicory.

At the age of eleven I went to Ribblesdale Senior School where boys and girls were separated. Football and cricket were played by the lads and hockey by the girls. We were all allocated to one of four houses: Hodder, Kemple, Pendle and Calder with colours red, yellow, blue and green. We did not have uniforms and competed against each other in sports. I was in Kemple, later becoming the Captain and from there, School Captain.

I got a new bicycle, a Hopper which only had one gear as we couldn't afford a bike with three gears. My friends George Speak and Arthur Pollard also got new bikes and as we were all interested in railway engines we often went off to try and spot the trains which ran through Clitheroe from Blackburn and onwards to Hellifield and Carlisle. These trains often had engines which had names, but what we really wanted was to see the engines which pulled the main line train from London to Glasgow. The nearest point was at Broughton, just north of Preston and so we made the journey on our bikes, twenty five miles each way. This was our Saturday ride.

Pinching apples from orchards was classed as a game of chance rather than theft. Grindleton Village, four miles outside Clitheroe was a lovely area for conkers; but close to the Chestnut trees was an orchard some distance from the farmyard and bearing beautiful red apples, which of course we tested. The following year, the three of us good friends remembered the apples and as we set out to collect the conkers, we also took a brown paper carrier bag. We filled the bag with about twenty gorgeous fruits and set off back home. There was a steep descent, about a hundred yards long into the village square and we were travelling at a fair rate of knots when the carrier bag broke and the apples set off independently. It must have been a peculiar sight to the villagers when the fruit came to a stop, but we had disappeared by then. Perhaps there is a moral to this story because I never again pinched another apple!

As the time to leave school quickly approached, I still had hopes of driving engines. However before that, you have to spend time cleaning the engines. As the nearest railway yard was in Accrington, I got an interview for a job and cycled over, hope filling my heart that I would get a position. As I was very fit, the physical tests went ok. My eyesight was good and I was given a colour test. This consisted of a number of different strands of wool and I gave a colour to each and rode back to Clitheroe thinking that all had gone well. Obviously it hadn't, as knowing now that I am colour-blind; I had probably messed up the colours of the strands of wool. I never heard from them, nor was I given the result of the interview. I assume that I wasn't suitable because of the problem I had with the strands of wool.

1937-1939

My father and his brother James, my Uncle Jim, were very close and my mother and his only daughter Winifred were great friends. We used to go to his home in Pendle View, Chatburn as often as possible. His grandson Raymond was only one year younger than I was. Uncle Jim came to see us and he offered me a job as a gardener with the intention that in due course I would be part owner along with his grandson Raymond. Pendle View Nursery was known as the best in the Ribble Valley with a stall on Clitheroe market. We accepted his offer and I started at 10 shillings for a five and a half day week. It was a large Nursery in a beautiful spot which was overlooked by Pendle Hill. A little brook ran down one side and just in front of the garden entrance it turned sharp left. There was a narrow wooden footbridge crossing the stream for pedestrians and as the stream turned and widened it became a ford for vehicles. The water supplied all the needs and a beech wood at the top end of the Nursery supplied all the leaf compost and moss for the hanging baskets. In front of the wood was an area similar to a field and each year a portion four inches deep was sliced off, made into mounds and the year after it was soil for the seeds and plants. There was a posh shed which Uncle Jim used as his office, then two large aviaries where he bred bullfinches and canaries and also three greenhouses. All year round there were sufficient flowers for marriage bouquets and funeral wreaths. He also grew potatoes and vegetables were also grown to sell on his market stall.

Aunt Janey worked part time and the foreman, Bill Bithell, who was about thirty years of age, had started as a boy. Sadly he had to join the army and was killed at Dunkirk. There were two other gardeners, both in their forties; John Norris who lived in Clitheroe and Arthur Goldsmith who lived in Whalley. Arthur was married to the eldest daughter of the Metcalfe family who lived in

Shireburn Lodge. He was also the consistent winner of fell races. We all travelled to work on cycles. A year later, Raymond joined us and he wasn't very interested, being somewhat pampered and his contribution to gardening was considerably less than mine. In spite of this, we did get on together.

During the two years from 1937-1939, life was busy. The Clark family left the Church of England and became involved and attached to the Plymouth Brethren, Gospel Hall in Manor Road, Clitheroe. At the age of fifteen, I and my two friends Arthur Pollard and George Speak joined them and we were baptised into the Chapel.

To learn office work, I went to evening classes twice a week at the Grammar School to study English and I also took a correspondence course with Bennett College, Sheffield. I joined the Royal Air force Cadets, the ATC; and one weekend we had a trip to North Allerton and went up in a Lancaster bomber. I did digging and tidying up in other people's gardens to earn some pocket money. Whilst at the Nursery I was earning £1 a week after two years.

In 1939, the Royal Engineers took over Low Moor Mill as a barracks. We still resided at 11 West View and Cecil was now seven years of age. Our front room was devoid of furniture although it had a nice fireplace. When a knock came to the door, I opened it and a very smart young twenty year old lady named Dorothy Cripps asked me if she could speak to mother. I let her in and mother agreed with her to let out our front room which she would share with her fiancé who was a Corporal in the barracks. Within a week, they were residents. Dorothy and another lady had both come up to Clitheroe from London and obtained jobs at the Post Office in Clitheroe. Dorothy was a counter clerk and her friend was a telephonist.

I was sixteen, tall, very fit, not unintelligent and polite, and also looking for a change of job. Two months later Dorothy told me that there was a vacancy at the Post Office. One of the three ex-grammar school boys was being called up for service in the Army. They were sorting clerks and telegraphists. Dorothy told me to apply and I got the job. The first two weeks was spent learning Counter work at Blackburn G.P.O. and being very good at mental arithmetic, it was easy balancing the books at the end of the day.

At Clitheroe G.P.O. we worked three shifts between 5am and 9pm. I soon understood the reasoning behind spending my first two weeks on the counter, as the first task at 5am was to peruse the previous day's sheets from the five counter staff and have the full balance of cash and remaining stock ready for the Manager when he arrived at 8:30am. The difficult bit was when it didn't balance and even a half penny had to be found. The rest of the shift was taken up with sorting the outgoing letters destined for anywhere in the world into the separate letter racks and bags for the parcels. The other part of the job was to take the telephone calls for the telegram boy to take out on his bike which could be seven or eight miles away in the outer villages. The sad part was when the telegram was from the War Office.

Postmen would then take the bags at different times down to the railway station and put them into the guard's van on the train which would be going either north or south from Clitheroe. For incoming mail, sorting was the responsibility of the postmen. My wage had now doubled, and an extra income on top of my wage was to do fire watch in the post office at 3 shillings a night. All postmen were asked to do this, but some of the postmen didn't want to do it; so the lad doing the early shift would take his place, sleep all night and collect the three shillings. I did it as often as I could. I got on well with all of the postmen; three of whom had small vans to go round the villages and farms as far as Newton, Slaidburn and Bolton-by-Bowland; so when I had a holiday period, I went with them. As I have mentioned before, my Uncle Tom had a milk round and Aunt Rachel helped him. For an extra sixpence pocket money, I used to do the Henthorne district milk round each Sunday morning so that they could go to church.

I was now eighteen and one day when I was in grandma's house talking to Aunt Rachel. She had just finished her day's work and said, "We have a new customer at a big house in Low Moor on the other side of the river, called Shireburn. A lovely Swiss girl lives there and sometimes she is in the kitchen and takes the bottles from me." I wrote earlier that the gardener Goldsmith had married the girl from Shireburn lodge, but at the time the name of Shireburn meant nothing to me. The name was soon to become very familiar and a great part of my life.

My duties at the Post Office frequently took me to the front counter department and one day when I had my back to the counter, I heard a quiet voice with a slight accent say to the counter clerk, "Are there any letters please for Shireburn?" I turned, saw Nan, and instantly fell in love. I found two letters, returned with them and received a lovely smile in return. I don't remember the conversation, but a week later we played tennis on the Castle courts. Our legs were covered with red grit, but I asked her if I could take her back to Shireburn. It was a lovely evening. We walked over Brungerley Bridge, through the grounds of Waddow Hall, picked up some eating chestnuts and followed the back driveway to the country lane, Waddington Old Road. There was a five barred gate which I opened, and then we leant against it looking back at Pendle Hill, each of us holding a tennis racquet, and I kissed her. If Nan had been writing this part of the story, I wonder what she would have said.

We wandered along the lane the half a mile to the Lodge gate, said goodnight and I watched her walk up the drive to Shireburn. We had become instant friends and I knew it was the start of a lasting relationship. Our first real day together was on the train to Blackburn. We sat on the grass in Corporation Park until it was time for first house at the cinema. We watched 'Danny Boy' and the theme tune has remained with me ever since. Nan was aware that the milk lady was my aunt and of her own choosing, she stopped attending the Catholic Church and joined us at the Gospel Chapel. One Sunday evening, after listening to a young Evangelist minister Ernest Woodhouse, she spoke to him and said she wished to be baptised and did so at the Chapel.

In 1942 my grandad Clark died, and soon after I was called up to join the Royal Navy as a telegraphist. Nan and I became engaged immediately.

Anne Maria Ammann-Lussi

Born in Lucerne in Switzerland, Anne Maria was the youngest child of Emil and Brigitte Amman-Lussi. She had three older sisters, Gretle, Paulette and Claire; as well as a brother Joseph whom she called Seppi. Her father was born in Germany in 1880 and although he was a naturalised Swiss, he did fight for Germany as a foot soldier in the 1914-1918 World War. He owned a marble quarry in Nidwalden and the family lived in a large house in Stans.

Anne went to a Roman Catholic school and subsequently went at fourteen years of age to the Convent College in Stans, which was the equivalent to an English Grammar school and where all the teachers were nuns. Seppi was a P.E. instructor for the Canton and his little sister spent much of her leisure time with him; swimming, skiing and mountain rock climbing.

On leaving college, she wanted to become a Customs and Excise Officer, so she went to Rome, and then to Paris to brush up on her Italian and French languages. On returning home in 1938, her father died and she was aware that she needed English to complete her languages. She would then have five languages in all; Swiss, French, Italian, German and English.

Early in 1939, Caroline Garnett, the wealthy wife of a mill owner advertised in a Swiss newspaper for a lady companion. Anne saw it and realised that it would be an ideal way of learning English. She applied for the post and got it. Incidentally, Anne was never able to yodel, but she had a best friend who was the daughter of the Mayor of Stans and both of them played the mandolin. She would never have left Switzerland if she had known that she would be away for more than six years.

Anne was met at a railway station in London by Mrs Garnett and travelled up to Clitheroe by train to reside with the Garnett family in their eighteen roomed Manor house, Shireburn. It was situated on the Yorkshire side of the River Ribble at Low Moor, a village in the borough of Clitheroe. She had a room at the rear of the home with a view onto the vegetable and fruit garden and a bedroom on the second floor above the main entrance with a view of Clitheroe Castle and Pendle Hill.

The Garnett's were a wealthy family and lived in Waddow Hall. One of their sons Newstead married Caroline Horsfall from a high society family in Liverpool and as a wedding present from his father, Shireburn Hall was built. Newstead and his younger brother had owned a very large cotton mill in Low Moor, but in the slump of the 1930's they lost all their money and became bankrupt. Caroline; who was already a millionaire when she joined the Garnett family, had very astutely kept her fortune away from them and retained her money. It seems that Mrs Garnett decided to call her new companion Annie, but when I met her later, I changed it to Nan and so I will refer to her now in that way.

Newstead and Caroline Garnett had eight children; three boys and five girls; but when Nan went to Shireburn, only one of them was still there. Helen Garnett was a middle-aged spinster who always had to be addressed as Miss Helen and it was she who lived with her parents at Shireburn. One of their sons was a Major in the Indian Army and their youngest son Richard was a Lieutenant Commander in the Royal Navy and was the Captain of a submarine. Another daughter married a doctor from Clitheroe named Cooper, and it is only in the last few years that I realised he had been our family doctor. The domestic staff used to reside at the house but in 1939, the cook, two housemaids and a gardener all lived in the village of Low Moor.

Nan was twenty one years of age; a very polite, attractive and intelligent young lady who already spoke four languages and was immediately liked by everyone with the exception of Miss Helen and so it remained until the end of the war in 1946. I can only surmise, but gather

24

that Mrs Garnett could speak French and so together with Nan's English from her school days, it must have been quite difficult for the first few months; but all the time Nan was learning our language.

The old Garnett couple were very dignified people, but apart from walking to St Paul's Church every Sunday, they didn't go out together very often, other than the odd visit to Clitheroe. Caroline and Newstead didn't have a car but Mrs Garnett hired a local gamekeeper as a taxi driver. She was also very fond of Bridge and when the Bridge party was not at Shireburn, then off Nan went with her to all the homes of the Upper Classes; Lady Clitheroe at Downham Hall, Lady Aspinall from Pendleton Hall, Colonel and Lady Bolton of Browsholme Hall, Barrowclough and many more in the Ribble Valley. Obviously, she didn't join in the games, but was left with the staff at different houses. She became friendly with the cook at Shireburn and was accustomed to dealing with all the luxurious types of food which ration book holders couldn't get such as salmon, game, venison and meat of all kinds. Nan helped the cook prepare meals and after the cook had left for home, she was able to prepare whatever Mrs Garnett required and also help with visitors. Miss Helen did nothing to help at all.

Lt Commander Richard Garnett, son of Newstead and Caroline, and his wife were frequent visitors and Nan would tell me what a lovely couple they were; but sadly on the 1st June 1939, Richard died in the submarine Thetis which was on trials in Liverpool Bay and sank. Conditions on board were very cramped, as 103 men were on board that day, only 69 of them being the crew. The other men were engineers from Cammell Laird who chose to stay on board for this maiden voyage. Problems occurred with the first dive and hundreds of tons of water filled the first and second compartments. The submarine nose-dived. The rescue was beset by bad timing and bad luck as well as bad judgement. The S.O.S. took three hours to reach the Navy H.Q. and the nearest rescue ship was hundreds of miles away. Aircraft reported inaccurate locations for the stricken submarine whilst all the time carbon dioxide levels on board were getting dangerously high. Fuel and drinking water were dumped allowing Thetis to raise stern first. Four men escaped through a hatch and another four died trying to do the same. A wire hawser was fixed round the sub, but this snapped leaving the Thetis to sink to the bottom. The remaining men gradually suffocated and the bodies of the remaining 99 men remained on the ship for four months until the submarine was salvaged. Richard Newstead Garnet was a Lieutenant Commander of the Royal Navy and Captain of H.M.S. Taku when he was invited aboard the new submarine the Thetis as an observer. The newspapers were filled with the tragic story.

This is an extract from the Clitheroe Advertiser and Times of Friday 19th May 1940…

'In memory of Lieutenant Commander Richard Newstead Garnett, Royal Navy, third son of Mr and Mrs Newstead Garnett "Shireburn" Clitheroe who was lost in the sinking of the submarine 'Thetis' in June last, a beautiful stained glass window, the gift of his parents was unveiled at St Pauls Church, Low Moor, on Sunday last.

In June 1939 a new class of submarine was having its sea trial and was named the 'Thetis' and departed at 10am and by 3pm had sunk 160 feet below the surface with the result that 99 men died including Lt Commander R N Garnett. 4 men survived. Lt Commander Garnett had been invited aboard the 'Thetis' along with other officers and workers from Cammel Laird at Birkenhead who had built the submarine. The 'Thetis' was raised 12 weeks later and rebuilt and renamed the 'Thunderbolt'. One diver also died as a result of raising this doomed submarine. The 'Thunderbolt' was sunk on the 14/3/1943 this time by an Italian Sloop named the Cisogna with 62 men lost this time.

Lt Commander Richard Newstead Garnett was in fact the officer in charge of his own submarine the Taku. We have information that the majority of those lost were buried in a mass grave at Holyhead. We do not as yet know if Lt Commander Garnett was buried with these men or returned to the Ribble Valley.'

Later in 1939 with England at war with Germany all the passports of aliens were checked and it was found that Nan held a German speaker's passport and consequently she was interned and taken to Port Erin on the Isle of Man where she was made to live for a few months at a small hotel with other lady occupants until clarification of her nationality could be established. All the female internees were placed in one row of hotels and boarding houses overlooking the sea and the males were all at the other end of the beach. It was a leisure period for Nan and being a good swimmer she spent a lot of her time in the sea. Fortunately others also swam because a sudden surge of water once took her further out and she was drowning when another swimmer realising her plight, managed to rescue her and get her back to the sand. She never did find out who he was. In spite of the leisure time, this wasn't a happy period in her life as there were no other Swiss people there as far as she knew and she didn't make any friends. Soon the authorities realised that she was Swiss and not German and so she was brought back to Shireburn. With the exception of Miss Helen, the family received her with open arms.

In 1939, Miss Helen was 44 years of age, a spinster and so had never married. She was used to ruling the roost over the staff until Nan's arrival. Mr Garnett absolutely adored his new arrival and so Miss Helen found her nose pushed out. Nan had no control over the staff, who were always polite to her. Once Nan and I were married, Helen seemed to alter for the better. Sometime in the 1960's she moved into a small house in Low Moor and named it 'Caraway Cottage'. I was then a Sergeant in Rawtenstall and we used to visit her occasionally, something which we continued to do until her death in 1985 when she was 91.

She was a well- known character in Clitheroe.

After the death of Richard Garnett; the favoured son of Newstead and Caroline; things must have been difficult. But life has to go on and as war was declared, things were extremely different. Switzerland was isolated and Nan was unable to go home. Low Moor Mill, having been empty for several years became the garrison of the Royal Engineers and remained so until the end of the war. The ½ mile length of land on the Yorkshire side of the River Ribble was owned by Mrs Garnett and this became a training ground for bridge and pontoon building for something like 700-800 troops. Some of the senior officers for a period of time slept at Shireburn, but had all their meals in the barracks. They had a lounge and so Nan had the additional job of brewing up for them if it was required.

There was a private drive from Shireburn of about 100 yards which led to the gateway on Waddington Old Road where there was a gatehouse. A family with four daughters lived there; the father working as a roadman for the Yorkshire Authority. It was his job to keep the two mile stretch of road between Edisford Bridge and Waddington tidy. Their eldest daughter Nellie was married to one of my uncle's gardeners at Chatburn Nursery.

Nan had a cycle which she often used and her route to Low Moor and Clitheroe took her out from the driveway, down a steep decline of 60 yards to a small path which led to a narrow wooden footbridge, and then across the river to the mill. The path then broadened out to a road 10 feet wide between the wall of the mill and a 3 foot stone wall overlooking the river. When the river was in flood, the water level rose to the bottom of the wall and level with the roadway. This mill road then covered two hundred yards up a slight incline into the village centre, all unlit. I can't think that Nan would ever have used it after dark. This was also the route I took after I met her.

With all the troop movement, Clitheroe became a very busy place; in particular Low Moor; and what had been a lovely spot on the river bank became a quagmire of mud. However, there was a large field which Garnett's owned on the south side of the house, with Bashall Brook running along one side of it and into the river. The old man kept ducks and hens in this field, and it was one of Nan's jobs to help him feed them daily and collect the eggs. This was something she really enjoyed doing.

Prior to the war, Nan used to get money from home, but that came to an end so all she had was the allowance which she received from the Garnett's. They realised this and it was agreed that she would be paid a proper wage for what she did. This is what happened: the cook, instead of working into the evening left before teatime but prepared the evening meal. Nan cooked it then served the meal to the Garnett's as there was no staff left in the building. Nan didn't mind this arrangement because she had always eaten the same as the family although never with them. The only bad part was washing up afterwards.

Every Sunday morning, the Garnett's walked to the local church of St Pauls, and Nan who was originally a Catholic either walked or cycled to the Roman Catholic Church in Lowergate, Clitheroe. She did sometimes visit the Post Office. Nan occasionally smoked the odd cigarette, always in a holder until after we met and although she would not have had much money, she always wore K shoes and was immaculately dressed. To this day in 2014, I can't understand how a girl so nice didn't fall in love until late in 1940, but she became part of my own life story and our love lasted for 51 years.

As I sit in my home now, and look across at the lovely photo of dear Nan which was taken the day she came to live at Shireburn, so many wonderful memories of our lives together come flooding back and I can't see for the tears.

The war years

Training and getting married

In 1942 aged 18 years, and employed as a sorting clerk and telegraphist in Clitheroe General Post Office, I was conscripted into the Royal Navy as a telegraphist. As I have mentioned already, it was at this time that I became engaged to be married to a young Swiss girl named Anne-Marie Amman Lussi (Nan). This obviously made the departure to my training all the more difficult as Mother, Cecil and Nan waved me off. It was the first time I had to leave everyone, so it felt sad but I was expected to return in due course after my training. However, I departed from Clitheroe railway station with a ticket to Skegness, changing trains in Manchester. In the same carriage were three men; John Worsley, son of an accountant from Burnley, Dick Thomas, a railway telegraphist from Crewe, and Cyril Tattersall, also a railway telegraphist from Failsworth. We became firm friends and stayed that way throughout all our training, firstly in Skegness, then Glasgow and finally Ayr on the Scottish coast.

We spent two months at HMS Royal Arthur where we learned the rudiments of seamanship and discipline. Then we went for thirteen weeks to HMS Shrapnel, an old mill in Rotten Row in a slum area in Glasgow city centre. In that mill was a Plymouth Brethren Chapel. To learn coding and telegraphy, I attended the Marconi Wireless School at the University. There was great competition as to who would become top telegraphist at the end of the thirteen week training. I won, having gained 100 percent in each test!

I mentioned the Gospel Chapel in the mill, and it was there that I attended the Sunday morning service each week. The congregation took a liking to me and took me back to their homes; some poor and living in tenement buildings and others who were well off. One family in particular, the 'Winnings', had a son who was a Police Sergeant. He had been serving in the notorious district of the Gorbals when a drunk hit him with a broken bottle and he lost the sight in one eye. Mr Winning was an engineer on the docks and I became the best of friends with the family and saw the sergeant quite often. One of the other parishioners was a tram driver and he took me all over the city including on a route which was fifteen miles long and cost 1p.

During my time in Glasgow, Nan bought a house back in Clitheroe and as we now had somewhere to begin our married life; we decided to get married on my first leave which coincided with my departure from Glasgow. This leave was for seven days commencing on the 1st of April, so we chose April the 2nd as the date for our wedding. She and my family made all the necessary arrangements and all I had to do was bring the best man with me.

The train from Glasgow to Preston would have arrived too late for me to catch the last train from Preston to Clitheroe, so Nan decided that rather than me staying all night on the platform, she would bring our two bikes to Preston so that we could cycle the eighteen miles home through the countryside during the night. She met my three friends as we arrived in Preston and Cyril Tattersall had elected to be my best man.

Part of the way home, we had been travelling quite quickly down a half-mile long steepish hill, when Nan started going quicker and quicker. I shouted, "Slow down!" to which she replied, "My brakes aren't working!" I knew that there was a sharp left hand bend at the bottom of the hill where there was a thirty foot drop into a stream. I pedalled as fast as I could, grabbed the seat of her cycle and managed to stop just before the bend. The beret she had been wearing flew off, but I found it a hundred yards back up the hill. We negotiated the last eight miles safely by walking the downhill bits. But why worry? We were together and had all night to get home. Nan slept that night at grandma's house and my Uncle Tom gave her away at our wedding.

We married on April 2nd 1943, (not April 1st as this was April Fools' Day of course), and this was just the start of a long and happy married life. Our reception was at a cafe which was lovely and later on that day, we caught a train to Morecambe to spend the first three days of our married life together. We stayed at a boarding house owned by two spinster sisters who had previously lived three doors away from us in West View. When we returned from Morecambe, our total assets amounted to 6d. Nan returned to Shireburn and as a wedding present, she was given a lovely Indian silver trinket box, and also; because she had married a sailor; three small picture prints which had belonged to their son Richard who had died on board the submarine Thetis.

After my leave was over, I went on to Ayr where our last two months of training was spent in a Pontins holiday camp – HMS Scotia… another ship with no water! Once training had been completed, I moved on to Devonport in Plymouth; one of the three main naval bases. I said my farewells to my pals, not knowing if we would survive this awful war, or even whether we would ever meet again. I went on to Plymouth, a place I had never seen before. There were enough of us to fill a lorry and we were deposited five miles later at Glen Holt, a signalling depot in the middle of a wood and on the edge of Dartmoor just off the main road to Tavistock. Before the war it had been a nudist camp. There were about two hundred of us, ordinary telegraphists, coders and signallers in Nissen huts, arriving and departing daily. Each morning we lined up and if your name and number was read out you knew it was firstly leave and thence to a ship. There was no mention of where the ship would be or the name, until you returned from leave.

Whilst I was at Glen Holt I met a very nice young man called Cliff Timson who was a Baptist and came from Hull and we remained friends for the six weeks until my departure. It was a leisurely period when we could go into

Plymouth each day on the lorries, provided we returned each day for the evening meal. Plymouth had been badly bombed and there was devastation everywhere. The Cathedral had received a direct hit and only the outer walls still survived with no roof other than a small portion mid centre of the North wall. The crypt had been resurrected and the N.A.A.F.I. used it, together with the WVS ladies as a refreshment room. Beans on toast with coffee cost just 3d.

As Cliff and I entered the N.A.A.F.I, I heard an amazing sound which I will remember to the end of my days. It was the sound of the organ in this ruined church and the organist was playing 'Handel's Largo'. Remarkably, the organ had only received minor damage. Fifty years later, Nan and I visited Plymouth; the old ruins remained but a new church had been built alongside. The ladies in the church shop were astounded when I told them my little story.

Across the Atlantic

Whilst at Glen Holt I found that I could take an exam to get to the next step up on the promotion ladder; ordinary telegraphist to telegraphist. Thirty of us took the exam but only two passed and I was one of the two. Eventually, in August 1943, the day arrived when I was told that I was going to Boston in the U.S.A. and my seven day's leave was granted. When I arrived back at Glen Holt around forty of us joined nine hundred other sailors on the railway platform at Plymouth and then onto a troop train which went overnight to Greenock. The 'S.S. Queen Elizabeth', the world's largest liner was anchored mid river and we were ferried out to her. There were already two thousand American troops on board. Within two hours we had set sail for New York. I distinctly heard the first message on the tannoy:

'No-one must get undressed on this crossing and life belts must be carried'.

At this stage, clarification is needed about life belts. Each British sailor was issued with an inflatable belt; fine if you had enough breath to blow it up before jumping into the water. Attached to it was a waterproof battery with a small red light bulb. (Ten years after the war I found mine in the garage and the bulb still lit up!) I couldn't swim, and though before I joined up I was never away from the River Ribble, I had avoided the deep bits, and my previous contact with the sea was paddling in it at Blackpool.

The Admiralty had decreed that large fast passenger liners would out-speed U boats, and it worked. They avoided the convoy routes, but even so there was some trepidation because we were all aware that torpedoes travelled at several times the speed of the fastest ships.

We set sail that night, unescorted across the Atlantic to New York. It was beautiful weather, and we moved at a top speed, hoping that the person who told us that we were too fast for U-boats to catch us, would be correct. The magnificent liner we had boarded was painted a dull blue/grey to blend with the ocean. Our cabin was in one of the lower decks and although it was a double cabin, space was limited as there were eight of us to share its restricted accommodation. We were able to wander about the ship throughout daylight hours and I realised that if there was a big bang in the night, the casualty count would be high as the journey to the open deck was a long one. Not a comforting thought, but my little prayer each night throughout my life must have helped. The weather was beautiful and all the Yankees on board were either throwing dice or sunbathing. I tried the latter and got sunburned! It taught me a lesson for life. I saw the Statue of Liberty as we approached New York, and then everything else was a vague memory until I woke up in the Naval Hospital in New York docks suffering from severe sunburn. The following day I was taken to join the rest of the crew.

Several days were then spent in a seaside resort outside the city, Astbury Park – the Blackpool of the New York day trippers, and it was there that I met up for the first time with the signaller's department. It really was a few days of leisure before boarding a train to Boston, to commission the Captain-class frigate, HMS Cooke - K471. We stayed in a large hotel on the beach and the sands stretched out into the distance. White people were here and there, but there was one exception. A 100 yard stretch of beach had a wire fence round it and about 400 black people of all ages were splashing around inside the wire. This was my first sight of American black and white segregation.

HMS Cooke

The HMS Cooke was built by a Boston ship yard and launched on 22 April 1942 and originally named USS Dempsey. It was sponsored by Mrs JA Dempsey, mother of US Navy Lieutenant John Dempsey who was killed in action aboard the heavy cruiser USS Vincennes when it was sunk by the Japanese in the Battle of Savo Island in 1942. It never sailed as a US ship but was handed over to the UK and re-named HMS Cooke. This name was in memory of Captain John Cooke who died commanding HMS Bellerophon at the Battle of Trafalgar on the 21st October 1805.

Up until this point, ship losses had been tremendously high and the U-boats were winning. Most of the convoys consisted of old and slow moving ships and the smoke from them could be seen fifty miles away. The Americans were building diesel engine frigates and cargo vessels, all welded instead of riveted. We were one of the first frigates named after American Admirals. Five other frigates joined us later to become the third Escort Group.

The crew of 156 met the Captain; Lt Commander Leonard Charles Hill O.B.E. R.N.R who had been one of the crew of 'Scott of the Antarctic' on the exploratory expeditions to the South Pole. There were three signallers, three telegraphists and three coders. On the first day aboard, the coder allocated to me was W.R. Harraway

(Zeb) and we remained together on the same watch throughout the two years on this ship. In charge of us was a regular R.N. Leading telegraphist who was Irish.

For several weeks we sailed daily on manoeuvres having to accept that we really were now committed to life at sea. These frigates were welded instead of riveted and instead of a keel all they had were stabilisers. Also, although we carried large numbers of depth charges, we were not fitted with torpedo tubes, which made us very much lighter than destroyers. The minutes when we left harbour and moved into choppy water became very uncomfortable, a feeling which I never got over throughout the two years. The ship became a 'bucking bronco' and we dreaded hitting the first real storm.

From the first day in the Royal Navy we had been issued with a hammock, which was then carted from place to place with the expectancy that one day we might sleep in it. To my delight and that of many others, we found that Americans were fond of comfortable surroundings and so everyone on board the Cooke had a bunk. Luxury! The only problem was that when the ship moved, so did everything else. The hammock was stored away until 1945. Another surprise was to find that we had coffee percolators, ice-cream makers, drinking water fountains and even a laundry. However, I received a shock to my system when I went to sit down in the toilets. I found ten 'thrones' all in a row, all in full view. This was rectified when we eventually got back to the UK, and a refit converted them to conform to British standards of privacy. However, we unfortunately lost the perks – the ice-cream, coffee and drinking fountains.

I kept away from the normal troop establishments and in Boston I found a large Baptist chapel, Tremont Temple and again I met some nice people, the McIlwraith family who looked after me throughout the next six weeks. It was a six mile tram ride to their beautiful home in Newton.

I was quite sad to leave Boston, but we then went in beautiful weather to the lovely islands of Bermuda and into the harbour of the capital, Hamilton for the final few sea trials. The docks in Hamilton were very small but we were able to berth in a narrow inlet alongside a narrow road which led into the town centre ½ a mile away. There were no motor cars, just bikes and horse drawn carriages. This time I made friends with the C of E vicar and his wife. The vicarage was on the edge of the beach in front of the beautiful blue ocean. I was going to lovely places but all the time I was wishing that I was with Nan.

For several weeks our routine was again a round of daily sailings into this beautiful, blue ocean, sometimes to the only other port – St George, where we anchored in the small bay and went into the town's landing dock by motor boat. The period in Bermuda was to allow the mainly young crew to adjust to battle conditions and the tactics used to get to grips with U boats. This is when we found that at full speed we were able to turn 180 degrees in half the distance it would take a destroyer. Compared to most warships, the armament (other than depth charges) was very light; 3x3-inch mark twenty guns, two facing forward, and one aft, and one Bofres gun and seven Oerliken guns for attacking surfaced U boats or aircraft. The calm ocean was useful for the learners but I felt very sorry for the pilot of a small aeroplane towing a drogue behind it (albeit a long way behind) because he was taking his life in his hands every time the guns were fired. A year later the gunnery, especially by the 3 inch crews, had improved no end.

There was great excitement when we were told we were going back home via Newfoundland, but little did we know what was going to happen. We were in a part of the sea, later known as The Bermuda Triangle, and we sailed into a storm of unmerciful ferocity. There was a large crash and a monstrous wave caught us side on. In the wireless office behind the bridge we couldn't see out but we knew that we were taking a pounding. Suddenly we were thrown off our chairs; the ship rolled onto its port (left) side then rolled over to the starboard (right) side. We went 61 degrees to port, then 60 degrees to starboard. Everything that was loose went in all directions. It was frightening, but we survived. A signalman on the bridge told us that the Captain and all the rest of the crew on the bridge thought we would sink and that no-one could have lived through it. Apparently 62 degrees was the turning over point to upside down which would mean the loss of the ship and all the crew. 62 degrees off centre was the maximum so we were only one degree off death!

The Captain and the deck crew saw the wave and just clung on to the nearest solid object and fortunately the helmsman held the vessel on course. There would have been no SOS call as Zeb and I were tossed over sideways on our chairs; left then right. Everything that was loose and could be broken was smashed, as it was throughout the ship. I could go on for page after page, but suffice to say, that only one of the crew received injury other than severe bruising and it happened to be a telegraphist who broke an elbow. This necessitated the two remaining telegraphists doing twelve hours duty each day until we reached Belfast, and by Jingo, were we tired! The Captain told us we had hit the tail end of a hurricane and said that he had been just as terrified as the rest of us.

It took us five days to reach the United States Naval base at Argentia in Newfoundland, and there was a shortage of food, not that anyone wanted much. The threat of disaster had robbed us of our appetites in spite of the large bunch of bananas hanging in the corner of the wireless office! These bananas had been purchased by a crew member hoping to enjoy the ripened bananas once we had returned to England. The bunch diminished daily and by the time we eventually reached Argentia, only about twenty of the one hundred were still there. No-one complained, so the mysterious purchaser was never known.

We were joined by the other five frigates and became known as the Third Escort Group. We were second in line which meant that we got all the sticky jobs. After two days of rest in extremely good conditions, repairing what we could and restocking the food supply, we joined a large convoy to the UK. It was a very mixed group of merchant ships capable of different speeds, but obviously it moved at the speed of the slowest vessel, some of which were belching black smoke which could be seen for fifty miles away. In mid- Atlantic we hit what became customary storms, during which one ship broke down and 'Cooke' had to go and find it. When we did, the convoy had disappeared and we found ourselves 'sitting ducks'. Fortunately, the ship resumed passage, but instead of doing what all convoys were obliged to do – zigzag to confuse the U boats, we had to take a straight course to catch up. It was only the stormy seas that saved us as we later found we had somehow avoided being seen by a wolf pack of fifteen U boats.

Two weeks later, we left the convoy off Northern Ireland and arrived in Belfast docks. It was to be our home base until the end of hostilities and we were joined by Escort Groups 4 and 5. It was wonderful to see the coastline and know we would go on leave while the ship had a refit, but I was disappointed when I found I would be in the second batch to go.

Something like a miracle then occurred. A Lieutenant came aboard; the sports and welfare officer from HMS Caroline the depot ship, and spoke to me.

"I understand you are a good footballer," he said. "We have a team which plays in the Northern Ireland Amateur League. Will you play for us whenever possible and would you be our Captain?"

Of course I said "Yes" and he then followed that with news which was a gift from heaven. He had arranged for Nan to come to Belfast and she was able to stay for a week in a hotel in the city centre. The following day Nan was given a rail ticket at Clitheroe station to Heysham to join the overnight ferry to Larne. When she finally boarded the ferry, Nan was told that all the sleeping accommodation was occupied. However, she was taken to the Captain who told her he would be on the bridge throughout the passage and that she could have his sleeping apartments. When the ferry docked at Larne she was brought by naval transport to Belfast and we had a wonderful seven days together. One day she came aboard the ship and we had a lunch in the Petty Officers' mess. Whilst we were in Belfast, we went to the Gospel Church and met an Irish family, Mr and Mrs Morrow and their twenty year old son. They took us home for a meal and when Nan visited Belfast a second time a year later, she stayed with the Morrow family and they let us have one of their bedrooms. After the war, this family became friends with my Uncle Tom and Aunt Connie and they visited each other's homes.

With regard to the football team, the depot supplied the boots and I never even knew the name of any team member, nor the ships they were from. I was twenty years of age and I can't remember if we ever won a match, but we played on some lovely Irish FA football grounds.

But now back to HMS Cooke and the third escort group. When we commissioned the ship in Boston a very small black and white kitten walked aboard from the dockyard, and the stokers looked after it for twelve months until it wandered off in Belfast and perhaps joined another ship. This little kitten became our mascot during its time on board and must have lost at least one of its nine lives during the hurricane.

The newly formed escort group, EG3 was comprised of four American built frigates, but due to the scarcity of frigates, two British corvettes made up the compliment of six escort vessels. The commanding officer was in H.M.S. Duckworth and our skipper Lt Commander Hill was second in command.

The first convoy was to Gibraltar, without incidents

other than the notorious stormy waters of the Bay of Biscay. We didn't even re-fuel at Gibraltar where we were joined by H.M.S. Blackwood and then returned to Belfast where we were given another arrival, H.M.S. Essington and the two corvettes departed. Sadly Blackwood was torpedoed. This event is covered later in my story.

The refit lasted a few weeks. All luxuries were disposed of other than the bunks and we were fitted with the latest radar, Asdic, and other equipment including metal tracks on the deck to enable depth charges to be transported aft much more efficiently. The additional weight both above and with the inclusion of more depth charges being stored, did help to stabilise the ship, but not by much.

We then went as a group to the Orkneys and became the anti-submarine screen for five warships which were due to be part of the new East Indies fleet, (three battleships and two aircraft carriers) and we were able to escort them to Port Said in Egypt. We hit some very heavy seas after leaving Scapa and our senior officer requested the faster larger warships to slow down a little as we were going flat out and were scarcely able to keep up, but the request was refused. Fortunately the Bay of Biscay wasn't as bad as the previous journey so we did reach Gibraltar, and this time we re-fuelled in the docks although we were not allowed ashore. We did however receive mail and as usual I received more than anyone else aboard. It always seemed remarkable that letters could precede us to many destinations, but what a joy to receive them.

In five days we travelled the length of the beautiful Mediterranean Sea to Port Said. I remember the first morning looking north and seeing in the far distance the snow topped Spanish mountains. We had to keep as far as possible from German occupied land in case of dive bombers and we arrived safe in Port Said to berth in the Suez Canal. The warships left us and we remained in Egypt for two days. We were given shore leave and of course were accosted many times by Arabs showing photos of their sisters who were available for a small sum; and I had great difficulty in stopping my coder Zeb, from wandering off with them.

Whilst in Port Said, the battleship HMS Ramillies arrived from the East Indian fleet. We escorted it back to England ready for it to take part in the D-Day landings. We returned to Belfast on the 27th January 1944.

Atlantic Escort Duty

Throughout February and March we were constantly in the Atlantic either escorting convoys or doing U-boat sweeps, hunting the known wolf packs. Sometimes we re-fuelled from an oil tanker in mid ocean which didn't help our food situation. After five days at sea we always ran out of fresh food and had to rely on reduced rations and whatever the cooks could invent. Biscuits were available but they were the ones generally called 'dog biscuits'.

During this period in mid Atlantic in a heavy storm, I saw a mile away, a large liner steaming at full speed towards America, its bow surging deep into the waves and spray sweeping back higher than our mast head. I have often wondered if any passenger saw us bobbing about like a cork and whether they thought they had seen a submarine.

Frigates were not fitted with deck rails, but there were metal stanchions welded to the deck with several strands of wire between them. In a very heavy storm, the wind howling, large waves sweeping the deck and in pitch darkness, Zeb and I came up from below to take the midnight – 4am watch. The Frigate was 88 metres long and the wireless office was a third of its length from the bow, the mess-deck door being two thirds the length, approximately thirty metres from the stern. We waited for the ship to roll in the right direction, opened the door then closed it. I climbed quickly up the six-runged ladder to the gun deck and reached the wireless office expecting Zeb to be behind me. He wasn't! Three minutes later he came into the office soaking wet and told me that he had been washed overboard. Apparently I had reached the upper deck and he was grasping the ladder when the next wave swept over the deck. He lost his grip and the wave took him overboard. Two things saved him: the ship was moving so slowly, almost dead slow, and he was wearing an oilskin. The coat kept him on top of the water and the following wave swept him back on board the ship, and he was able to grasp the very end of the depth charge rack which overhung the stern and he scrambled back to safety. He did the four hours duty but we decided not to tell anyone and not to discuss it as he could well have been in trouble for not taking more care. If he had been drowned, this would have left me without a decoder making the job of receiving and decoding messages more or less impossible until such time as a replacement was found. A decoder from another watch would have had to be brought in to take his place. Meanwhile if an urgent message had arrived, it would not have been decoded immediately which could have been a life or death situation. We had both been through the hurricane in Bermuda and knew how close we had been to death, but that short period overboard must have been absolute terror for Zeb.

Another incident arose as the ship was returning from mid-Atlantic in an extraordinarily calm ocean. One morning a crew member was reported missing. The ship was searched but there was no trace of him. He was employed by the NAAFI as the manager of the small shop aboard the ship. The investigation was dealt with by a Sub Lieutenant who was a London Metropolitan policeman. The only information he received was that the man had been seen the previous evening. We were one hundred miles from Belfast and his death was recorded as 'lost at sea'. The officer's enquiries revealed that there were discrepancies in the books, and also that some of the crew didn't like the way he dealt with the cigarette and chocolate rations. Nobody falls overboard in a very calm sea, unless pushed!

Off the coast of France we found a German mine thirty yards away from us and we came to a very quick stop. With our shallow draft, we never knew whether we were in a minefield or whether it was an odd mine from a U boat. It was certainly necessary to explode it, but it took over an hour. The gun crews used rifle fire to hit the tip of one of the prongs, but from a fair distance away, that wasn't easy. However there was a tremendous explosion when it detonated and we cleared off in quick fashion.

A different type of incident arose one day in a very heavy storm. We were in our usual position on the left of a convoy when a message was received in the wireless office from the bridge…

'Why is the convoy all moving right whilst we are going straight on?'

I looked down and saw that the plug had come out of the wireless set, and I had missed an urgent message to turn to starboard. When we reached base I was in front of the Captain and received two days 'jankers' red-leading the bilge of the ship. A terrible job which taught me a lesson!

Invasion!

On April 5th 1944 the Group returned to Belfast where it was found that our engines needed maintenance in preparation for the invasion of France. Something happened and the engine room was flooded and it took four weeks to dry out. As a result, we all got ten days leave.

In early June, the Group now seven strong, sailed down the Irish Sea to Milford Haven in the Bristol Channel, where we joined numerous other ships. It was a virtual overspill for the Channel ports which were packed to capacity. Back then no-one knew the invasion date, but we now know that it should have been June 5th. However, bad weather prevented the invasion troops from reaching France and after setting off, the stormy weather caused them to return. A sudden decision was made to invade the following day but although EG3 sailed at top speed with a convoy, we did not reach our destination in the western screen until June 7th – D-Day plus one.

We now came under the control of Captain Walker, who was C.O. of the 2nd Escort Group based in Liverpool and the top submarine killer in the country. The two groups made up the Western screen, approximately fifty five miles in length, the job being to prevent U-boats and the very fast E-boats from attacking the troop ships. EG3 were the ships nearest to France off Cap de la Hague near Cherbourg covering the distance back to Portland Bill near Weymouth. For several days there was no sign of the enemy ships so Captain Walker decided he would use a decoy (sitting duck) to tempt the U-boats. Cooke was the ship and we sailed closer to Cap de la Hague. There was no reaction from the Germans but we did save the life of a British spy. He had been living in the Cherbourg area, a fact that the S.S. knew so they were searching for him. He saw our ship, stole a canoe and paddled out towards us. Our motor boat met him and he and his canoe were brought aboard. He stayed in the Captain's cabin until we could deposit him back in England and the canoe was tied up outside the wireless cabin. The Skipper received the canoe from the spy in return for services rendered, the spy not knowing that his actions would be instrumental in saving the ship and all the crew aboard it.

Earlier in my story, I mentioned HMS Blackwood which joined us in Gibraltar. She was now sent to Portland to refuel and when she returned we were sent to Portland to drop off the British spy, and to refuel whilst we were in that harbour. H.M.S. Blackwood then took over our position and just four hours later she was torpedoed by U764 and sank. Fifty seven of the crew lost their lives and another fifty were injured. The survivors were picked up by the 'Essington' whilst 'Duckworth' and 'Domett' went after the U boat. They made contact and attacked the submarine, but although it was badly damaged, it limped back to Brest.

On 26th June the Second and Third Groups sailed to Cherbourg and help was offered to the US army who were fighting for control of the port, to shell the German positions; but the US Commander refused as the two sides were too close. On June 29th we sank U988 off Guernsey. We stayed in the Channel and the Bay of Biscay and on the 26th July we sank U 214 off the Eddystone lighthouse. U 214 had been in commission for several years and had sunk many ships including a warship and an American submarine whilst in the Pacific.

We returned to the Bay of Biscay where two of the Frigates sank a U boat off St Nazaire, but on 22nd August we returned to Belfast after being released from Channel duties and returned to convoy escort in the Atlantic and sweeping for submarines.

Arctic Convoy duty

In October 1944, whilst we were in Belfast, we received a stock of warm winter clothing, including a leather jacket and we realised that we were going on the Russian convoys which obviously meant a perilous journey. Our group of five frigates sailed line ahead up through the Inner Hebrides, passing many different Scottish Islands with beautiful scenery, arriving in Loch Ewe on the 19th of October. We entered the inner Bay to re-fuel then berthed at a jetty in a most inhospitable spot. There were no buildings, just a narrow rough road leading round the Bay towards a group of buildings about a mile away. The only movement was that of sheep grazing on the hillside.

We had been informed that we could go ashore and as I was accustomed to writing to Nan since our marriage in 1943, and with the hazardous journey ahead of us, I thought perhaps it might be my last letter. I put a few endearing sentences together with the hope of finding a post-box on shore. Zeb my coder and I were the only two to get off the ship and off we wandered. The buildings turned out to be a few offices and cottages – no red post-box in sight! I popped my letter through a rather large letter box in the front door of one of the offices, just in the hope it would find its way home! As it happened, Nan did get my letter, censored by Customs and Excise at Loch Ewe. On the way back to the ship we had a wonderful view of all the ships in the convoy. Forty years later, Nan and I toured up the West coast of Scotland, and we went especially to Loch Ewe. It was springtime and what a beautiful place it was.

We then joined a large convoy JE 61 for Murmansk. The 8th Escort Group consisting of one destroyer, two sloops and two corvettes were already there. We sailed North on the 19th October and were joined by the 15th and 21st Escort Groups, Aircraft carriers 'Vindex', 'Niarana' and 'Tracker', the cruiser 'Dido', the 17th destroyer flotilla and six US submarine chasers for the Soviet Navy.

It was slow going for several days due to the heavy weather, but then progress was made until we reached the Arctic Circle somewhere around the 73rd parallel. There was information that U boats were waiting for the convoy, so the third Escort Group and one of the aircraft carriers 'Vindex' were sent thirty miles ahead. As we reached Bear Island, the direction finding operators heard the noise of U boats conversing with each other and it turned out to be the Panther Group; nineteen submarines in all. We came into contact with them but I understand that due to the water temperature it was very difficult to pinpoint their position. They fired many torpedoes but because of our quick change of direction, the Group were all able to avoid them and we kept them under water to enable the convoy to sail intact into Kola Inlet on the 28th October.

On 31st October the wolf pack were again waiting for us so the 3rd, 15th and 21st Escort Groups were sent ahead to clear the path for the returning convoy RA 61. We again made contact, but unfortunately one of the Frigates in the 15th Escort Group, H.M.S. Mounsay was hit by a torpedo. Eleven lives were lost but another Frigate was able to get her back to Kola Inlet to be repaired.

Convoy RA 61 sailed on the 2nd of November and headed for the UK and once again we were 'in the van', but were heading for home! My 21st birthday was on the 4th of November 1944, and that was the day when Escort Group three was detached to rendezvous with a fast convoy JE 61A heading for Russia, which consisted of two large liners, S.S. Empress of Australia and S.S. Scythia escorted by a cruiser an aircraft carrier H.M.S. Campania and the 23rd destroyer flotilla. During this transition we encountered very heavy weather. The liners were carrying 11,000 Soviet troops who had been captured by the Germans and forced under duress to fight for them. They were being repatriated to Russia where we arrived on the 6th November in Kola Inlet.

I have spoken often in my narrative about the tremendous waves in mid-Atlantic and the Bay of Biscay and although the Arctic waves were not as big, we swooped from swell to swell, shuddered and tossed as the prow dipped under the waves and the propellers were often out of the water. We encountered the icy conditions of winter in the Barents Sea. Icy water sluiced the deck and spray formed as ice on the metal stanchions and wires, and it became a treacherous passage to and from the wireless office. It was of course very warm inside the vessel but I have often heard from people like me who aren't true sailors, that if you feel unwell it is better to be outside than inside.

Sanctuary in Kola Inlet was a relief from what might have been a disaster. Royal Navy ships were not allowed in Murmansk so we had to berth in an isolated spot which had an icy, snowy and extremely barren outlook. However, we were close to a small town and Zeb and I went ashore. There were no men about, but plenty of women and children. All the women were slim and very well dressed in furs including wonderful fur-lined leather boots. I did notice a small post office, but as we had no Russian currency, we postponed our visit there until another day.

In the centre of the town and situated right in the middle of the street were the public toilets. They were within a circular structure which had a roof and twelve cubicles, each open to the elements. Each cubicle had a small wooden door which just about preserved the modesty of the occupier, having a gap at the bottom where the feet could easily be seen, and a gap at the top where the head was also visible. The inside was really a little pit where the occupier crouched and made his or her 'deposit'! Both male and female users were treated the same and no special cubicle was reserved for either.

From being a small child, I saved foreign postage stamps, so on our second visit into the town, I carried with me a Mars bar and two bars of soap and went into the post office. A girl in her early twenties was the post mistress and when I produced the chocolate and soap, she realised that I wanted stamps! She eagerly took the luxuries from me and in return she stuck ten stamps on a Russian document and date-stamped them, the 7th November 1944. They are still the pride and joy of my stamp collection.

As I returned to my ship, I saw a Russian submarine berthed next to us, and that night was the noisiest I had ever heard on our ship. We weren't allowed on the Russian ship, but they all landed on ours, complete with vodka, which then interchanged with the rum aboard 'Cooke'. Dancing was a cross between the Hornpipe and Cossack style, accompanied by mouth organ and accordion. The officer of the Watch never came near, so perhaps there was an officers' party at the front end of the ship!

On November 10th the third Escort Group left Kola four hours ahead of the returning convoy of liners and warships to clear the passage for the quick return to the UK. On the 13th, off Norway, we saw a German spotter plane but two planes from the aircraft carrier shot the shadowing aircraft down. On the 14th November the cruiser, carrier and the destroyer escort left us to return to Scapa Flow and we became close escort to the liners. At 1am in the morning, H.M.S.Duckworth asked us what the radio echo was which was coming from very close to us and the liners. Because of our bow wave our operator had missed it. It was a U boat on the surface but immediately we headed towards it, the U boat dived. We dropped a depth charge which prevented it from firing torpedoes and it dived deeply. We were the only close escort for the liners so we got them away quickly. We took them through the Minches into the Irish Sea and left them in the Clyde Estuary and returned to our Belfast base on the 16th November.

That was our final duty with convoys. For the rest of the war, we were searching from the English Channel up to Scotland as U boats were penetrating the coastal regions; in fact for two weeks, twice daily, it was necessary for 'Duckworth' and 'Cooke' to escort the Larne to Stranraer ferry. Several more U boats were sunk by Escort Group 3, but we received no individual credit.

Coastal 'sweeps' and VE Day

In December we did our last sweep in the Bay of Biscay in very rough weather and we were in our usual position, the closest to the land. I heard for the very first time, our three inch guns firing. A cargo vessel sailing close to the nearest land which was France, did not acknowledge our recognition signal, and thinking we were a submarine commenced firing at us, so we retaliated and several shells hit the vessel. The foreign vessel's wireless officer must have been very slick, as within minutes I took a message from the U.K. – 'E.G.3 please investigate neutral ship being attacked by submarine'. We realised it was us and the firing stopped. The C.O. of the group told us to deal with it and we went alongside. It was a Portuguese coastal ship, badly damaged externally, but there were no injuries other than shock, particularly to the wireless officer. One shell had penetrated the wireless room, but instead of exploding, it broke in two.

Our next instructions were to take the ship to England for repairs. The other ships went back to Belfast and we, at slow speed, escorted the Neutral back to England and on Christmas Eve in 1944 we sailed into Liverpool. Our skipper said that anyone living within three hours of Liverpool could have three day's leave; so on Christmas Day, Nan and I were at home together.

I have mentioned meeting Cliff Timson and becoming friends with him in Glen Holt, but little did I know that for two years he was also based in Belfast in the 5th Escort Group. A device named 'Hedgehog' had been invented to sink submarines and both my ship and Cliffs were to test it. Instead of going full speed and dropping depth charges, this invention worked in an entirely different way. We were to approach the submerged submarine at a very slow speed then fire eight small charges which would fall in a circle and then surround the submarine and explode. There was an almighty explosion from Cliff's ship which tore it apart. The bombs had gone straight up then down, so the bridge, wireless office and forecastle were blown to bits. A third of the crew died including Cliff. The ones our ship had fired worked but we were never able to sink a submarine with them.

When V.E. Day arrived, we sailed into Portsmouth and Zeb and I went to Bognor Regis. The Group finally returned to Belfast on May 29th 1945 and soon three of the Frigates; Cooke, Domett and Berry, sailed together from Belfast round the North of Scotland, down the North Sea to Hull where the crews left them. HMS Cooke was destined to be scrapping metal. When I left the ship for the last time, I turned back feeling very emotional, and looked at her without pennants or flags and I thought, 'what a wonderful little ship'. I still have a photo of H.M.S. Cooke hanging on my wall, and looking at it fills me with pride.

I have read somewhere that British sailors viewed the Frigates with trepidation, wondering how they would stand up to all that the Atlantic and Barents sea could throw at them, as well as enemy action; and I can tell them; extremely well!

We went back to Glen Holt and within days I became

the senior member of the Signals branch on a new frigate, the H.M.S. Wigtown Bay which was also in Belfast. We were told that we would be at the forefront of the invasion of Japan. The ship was bristling with anti-aircraft guns. I can't remember the name of any other crew member. We set sail for the U.S.A. but part of the way across the Atlantic, the atom bombs were dropped. The war was ended and we turned back. It was highly unlikely that we would have survived the Japanese invasion and so once more God was on my side.

Demobilisation and home…

I had no time to say goodbye to the people I knew in Belfast, other than the 'Morrows' and off we went back to Devonport. I was assigned to the signal office in the dockyard where I was on twenty four hours continuous duty, then two days off. I was in digs just outside the dockyard where a middle aged lady looked after four of us and we all called her 'Ma'. She made some wonderful clotted cream. One of our duties was hauling up the Royal Ensign at reveille. De-mobilisation started almost immediately but this depended on the time in service and I was several months off. Eventually my day arrived and I collected my little suitcase containing clothes; a suit, hat, shirt and tie, shoes and a mackintosh. On a lovely warm day I shuffled along a queue a hundred yards long until I could board the train for Manchester. Touts were offering £30 for the clothes, but I kept hold of mine.

I can't describe that journey home, just one of sheer delight. I can vaguely remember a nice looking Wren sitting opposite me as far as Bristol and talking to me. She said she was going home to Cardiff. The mail train from Manchester to Clitheroe was at 4:15 am. When I finally arrived home on the 8th May 1946, I was greeted at 1 Mitchell St by Nan with our five week old son Ray, and a bundle of wool which was either going to kiss me or bite me, I wasn't sure which; but turned out to be our cross breed Old English Sheep dog, 'Tache'. Ray had been born in a private nursing home in Wilpshire and I had been allowed leave home from Devonport.

I previously mentioned a family friend of mine, Walter Clayton. He had been a friend of mine in St James Infant School and also Ribblesdale School. We both went to Sunday School and although his singing was not up to much, he used to sit in the choir next to me in spite of the fact that he used to keep quiet. When he was fourteen or fifteen, he was often with a farmer's daughter and football became a sort of 'one-off' for him. When I joined the Royal Navy, he became a paratrooper in the Army and when I was finally demobilised and returned home, I asked my mother if she had seen anything of Walter. Her reply shocked me as she told me he was dead. I was told that he had met a W.A.A.F, had an affair and one day taken her on the sands then killed her. He had been arrested, found guilty and hanged. In later years my thoughts returned to his predicament knowing that two friends could be so different: one a policeman and the other a murderer. This is the story as reported by 'True Crime'.

'Despite the grim austerity of post-war life in Britain in 1946, Joyce Jacques, a pretty 22-year-old brunette, was determined to enjoy herself. She had done her bit - joining the WAAFs at 18 and rising to the rank of Flight Sergeant. Now she wanted some fun.

When she met Walter Clayton, also 22 and recently demobbed, it didn't seem to matter that he was married. They began an intense and passionate affair during which Clayton spent every night at her lodgings in Morecambe, Lancashire.

During the evening of April 10th they had a quarrel, and Joyce thought about leaving him. They soon made it up, and on APRIL 12th, a Friday, they went on a pub-crawl, calling at five different pubs, starting with The Battery and finishing in The Elms.

Clayton was later to say: "Joyce felt a little drunk, so

we decided to go for a stroll along the front. We had a quarrel and I strangled her with my silk scarf. I left her on the beach and carried on by taxi to The Battery."

After another drink he went to the Central Pier, looking for his wife, who was out for the evening dancing. When he found her they went for a walk, and Clayton told her all about Joyce and how he had just killed her. He said that his wife then "asked me to go home with her for the last time."

The body of Joyce Jacques was found within an hour of her death, lying on the foreshore near a bus stop, just under the sea wall. Six hours later Clayton was charged with her murder.

He pleaded guilty at Manchester Assizes on July 16th, and in what must have been a near-record time for a murder trial - just three minutes - he was sentenced to death. He was hanged at Walton Prison, Liverpool, on August 7th, 1946.'

Nan had left Shireburn and I was left without a job and after discussing the Police as a profession, I got an application form from Lancashire Constabulary and took the examination in Clitheroe Borough Police Station. I signed on at the labour exchange and received 'dole' money for a few weeks which was only just enough to keep us. Nan had been away from her family in Switzerland for seven years so our priority was to go and see them on holiday.

1946 – The Police Force Beckons!

Police Constable, Liverpool 1946-1947

After our wonderful holiday in Switzerland, Nan and I returned home. Ray was four months old and when we arrived home, there was a letter waiting for me asking me to go and join the City Police force in Liverpool. I reported to Dale St Police station where I mingled with nine Liverpudlians, a Cockney and a Cumbrian; all ex-servicemen. We were taken to the City Hall where we took the oath to 'Save the King and Country'. We were measured for our uniforms and told to report to the Police Training School at Bruche, Warrington.

On the following Monday morning after a two hour bus drive from Clitheroe to Manchester, then a train from Victoria station en-route to Liverpool, I alighted at Bruche Station and walked to the rear entrance of the training school. Part of a United States bomber airfield, it was made up of Nissan huts which became my five and a half day lodgings each week for the next thirteen weeks.

The class was twenty seven strong, twelve of whom came from Liverpool, thirteen from Manchester and two rather nice policewomen from Hull. There were many other classes from all the northern forces, and being winter, they had a football team which I immediately joined. I was also the best table tennis player! It was hard graft to grasp the rudiments of police law in the three months available, but to me it was worthwhile and the discipline side was no trouble.

The officer in charge of the school was a Superintendent from Derbyshire, a very competent policeman. The second in command, Chief Inspector Sephton from Lancashire was a very dapper man, a white handkerchief always peeping out from under his left sleeve. He came in very handy when I dislocated my left thumb playing football, and he took me to Warrington

Infirmary to have it set. Twenty Five years later he became Chief Superintendent in Bury Division whilst I was an Inspector in Heywood and he hadn't altered; the little white handkerchief was still sticking out from his sleeve. Someone had to be a figurehead! Everyone at the training school passed out as a Probationary Constable, knowing that within two years, someone would decide either to keep you or give you the sack.

I reported for duty at Dale Street Liverpool and received the number E 187, then taken to Walton Police Station. None of the other eleven men were in E division and nine of them I never saw again. The nine Liverpudlians obviously lived with their families, but the rest of us were taken to a very large hostel in Kirby, until police houses could be found. It was two miles beyond the city boundary and full of university students. Our transport to and from work was a police van driven by a lady civilian driver. There were six of us in the van and I was the nearest to Kirby, so I was the first to be dropped off but the last to be picked up on the return trip.

Most unusually for police forces, Liverpool worked the three shift system, but starting one hour later: 7am – 3pm; 3pm – 11pm; and the night duty 11pm – 7am. We worked for seven days and the eighth day was our day off. When it came to the weekend, work ended on Friday at 3pm and the next duty was at 11pm on Monday which gave me more time at home with my family. It was quite a trick to reach home. It was a two mile walk along a country lane to the tram terminus at Fazackerly, then a tram to Aintree, the train to Preston and then the local train to Clitheroe. My weekly laundry was carried in a haversack.

In 1946, the police wage was £5 a week, plus a house allowance which in my case covered my time at the Kirby Hostel. Being a sportsman, I enjoyed my time at Kirby. I played volleyball, badminton, and joined the table tennis team which played in the Liverpool League. I also commenced playing for the Liverpool City Police F.C. when not on a rest day at home. They played in two leagues; a Wednesday local league, and on Saturdays the 'I Zingari' league – one of the best amateur leagues in the country. I played inside left and for the first time in their history we won the I Zingari league and were finalists in the Liverpool Amateur Cup. At the presentation of the trophies I received a very nice compliment, and the Deputy Chief Constable, Mr Martin, who watched all our matches, came in very handy later on when I needed to be transferred.

As Police Constable E187, I was taken to the E Divisional headquarters on Westminster Road. The southern boundary, the notorious Scotland Road was the worst area in Liverpool. West were the docks up to the Bootle City boundary; north was the Walton section up to Aintree and Fazackerly; and east was the East Lancs Road from Manchester. The Superintendent gave me a welcome talk and I never saw him again.

A senior constable then accompanied me to the dock road, also a very busy tram track, and he supervised me on point duty, complete with white gloves at a very busy junction, one road of which entered the docks. I had all my work cut out controlling the traffic, but I must have done alright as the bobby was satisfied. I was quite intrigued by several boys hanging about outside the dock gates as they were all carrying bags, then I realised they were waiting for Tate and Lyle lorries carrying sacks of sugar. Each lorry had to stop at the dock gates, but when it slowly set off they would slit one of the sacks and collect as much sugar as possible before the lorry sped away. My companion wasn't a bit interested, but on reflection, he wouldn't have been fast enough to catch them.

Back at Walton, the senior station Sgt handed me a small booklet showing the area of the three Walton beats and I was allocated number two beat which was the largest. It stretched from Breeze Hill, alongside the Bootle City boundary to Aintree and Fazackerly in the north and the East Lancs Road in the East. Walton hospital and the front of Walton jail were inside the beat; also a large cinema, a large coal siding, and an area of houses which would now be classified as slum; but there were very few shops. The main A59 from Preston to Liverpool ran through the centre which was also a double tram track. The southern edge of my beat was number one beat which contained most of the shopping area of Walton, including the bombed and derelict Walton Church. Everton and Liverpool football grounds were just beyond the far end.

I was then given some very sound advice:

'Liverpudlians – if they don't behave they expect to be clouted, but you don't complain if they hit you back!'

Another morsel of advice was: 'If you deal with a domestic quarrel, don't turn your back.' It would seem that a 6 months pregnant lady rang in to say that her husband had just kicked her in the stomach. The recruit who went to deal with it found the lady holding a large heavy pan, so he felt justified in knocking the husband down. Unfortunately he turned his back on the wife who then belted him on the shoulder with the pan shouting, "Lay off my husband!" The Sgt didn't tell me what happened next.

I was also told that if I saw the blue lamp outside the police station flashing, to get there quickly. As in all forces there would be a certain point on the beat which the street Sgt would allocate, where if at all possible we should be at the end of each hour. I have spoken about the very busy tram track, but at night the trams didn't run. If the Sgt tapped the tram line at night, it would be heard for a distance of half a mile; a signal which meant we had to walk back towards him. I was never with him for more than a few minutes. What on earth he did with his time I never knew. I can't remember his name or what he looked like.

In that first week at 10pm, I saw the blue light flashing and ran quickly to the station. There was a Working Men's Club about 100 yards from the station, and a man had provoked six others to the extent that they had attacked him. He had escaped by running down the street and entered the police station, then joined the station sergeant behind the front counter; quickly followed by the six other men. Regardless of the sergeant's presence, the men attacked their victim. Fortunately there was a detective constable in the back room who helped as much as he could, but they were tremendously pleased when they saw me. The police prevailed and there were six bodies, all conscious but some only just! The loner was no use; he just cowered in a corner. I never found out what happened to the six after that as my transport arrived to take me back to Kirby.

Another incident occurred in the first few weeks. There was a battle royal going on in the main street. A circle of onlookers was watching a number of men fighting. I dived into the fight to find the main combatant, a man with one leg and two crutches, one of which he was wielding with great effect. I managed to stop the battle and calmed them down. I really should have arrested the chap with the crutches, but common sense said 'leave him alone'.

I was three hundred yards from the police station when a tram heading towards Aintree stopped alongside me and the driver got out and said that the conductor and passengers were having a tough time with a violent drunk. I went aboard and handcuffed him. I asked the driver to carefully reverse the tram back to the police station and he agreed. This was a first for the station Sgt: a drunk arriving on a tram!

The same thing happened a second time; a drunk on a tram, but on this occasion I was in the transit van on my way back to the digs with five other officers aboard and the tram driver waved us down. I was the one who dealt with him but this time we took him back in the van which meant we were an hour late getting back to the hostel. Drunks always plead guilty in court, so it isn't necessary to give evidence.

The years 1946 and 1947 had very cold winters and the winter of 1947 was especially cold. The wind howled up the Mersey and even with my greatcoat and cape, it was very difficult to keep warm. We were all issued daily with a cod liver oil capsule and I don't remember anyone going off sick with a cold. I certainly never felt ill, but probably my experiences and 'conditioning' in the Royal Navy helped. There were always road works and sitting next to the watchman in his hut with a glowing brazier in front of it, was always welcome around 4am in the morning. They were usually men in their sixties and seemed to enjoy the company. I know that I did.

I was soon to catch my very first criminal. It was a very cold winter's night at about 2am. I was wearing my heavy greatcoat, plus the cape. The night sky was full of stars; one to remember if you are indoors in the warm. I was at the extremity of my beat, next to the tram track and at the hour point where the sergeant had chosen for me to be at hand. I was leaning on a five barred gate, the entrance to a very large coal siding. It was deathly silent and still, when suddenly I saw a movement thirty yards away. A man dressed in black ran out of the coal dealer's office. I vaulted over the big gate and went in pursuit. He ran up and down several coal dumps, over a double track railway line, over a fence, across some allotments, over another fence, down an embankment, across a main line and up the other embankment; at which point I dived and caught his leg. I had just enough energy left to handcuff him. I don't remember doing it, possibly before I vaulted the gate, but at some stage I pulled the chin strap down as I still had my helmet on.

I led him back to the main road and then the realisation that we could have been killed hit me. We had crossed the main line which was electrified and the live rail was between the wheel tracks. I then had a three quarter mile walk back to the police station; the two of us covered in coal dust and the only difference being that I had a uniform on. I then found out that he was a sailor on leave. He had broken into the office and was tackling the safe when he happened to look out and saw me looking into the yard. If he had not run, I would never have known he was there. He was charged with breaking and entering with intent to steal.

There was a large cinema on my beat, behind which was a back lane which was used once a week to play dice. Cinemas along with churches were the most eerie of places, especially during darkness and when they were left insecure. A gang used to throw dice against the cinema wall and bet on the result. It was illegal gaming and although I tried to catch them on many occasions, I was never successful. I later found that my miserable attempts were due to the fact that they paid children to inform them if a policeman came within a quarter of a mile.

The large Walton hospital was on the main A59, and the entrance was not far from the police station. I was never called upon to help them, but the student nurses were allowed out provided they returned before the main gates were locked at night. A security guard was also on duty on the gatehouse. If they were late, they were expected to report to the guard, but they would be disciplined, so with great difficulty they usually tried to climb the 5 foot wall. It was always on the same night of the week and I tended to be around to give them a 'leg-up'. This always earned me a lovely smile.

I mentioned three beats. The other two bobbies had two to three years' service. Bill, the bobby on beat number one lived a quarter of a mile from Walton Police Station. The beats all converged at a bowling green with the normal shelter. It was always quiet between 4 and 5 am, so we three used to meet at the shelter to have a chat, or sometimes we went for a cup of tea at Bill's house in the knowledge that the sergeant was never about at that time. Like most people, I used to spend a few coppers trying to win some money on the football pools, but when I saw the hundreds of part time checkers heading for Vernon's or Littlewoods buildings every Sunday morning, I gave up trying.

Liverpool and Everton football grounds were close and I did duty quite often at both grounds. Liverpool was then in Division two, but Everton were in the top flight. A lot of spectators rode pedal cycles to the match and were allowed to park them beneath the stands. One Saturday I was walking underneath the stand; I think it was Liverpool Cop, and I heard the half time whistle blow. There was the sound of running water, and gallon upon gallon streaming down the back wall. It wasn't rain water! There must have been at least a hundred peeing against the wall on the top deck! It was drenching all the cycles stacked below. This must have gone on every match day.

This reminds me of another incident about urine... In the middle of a summer's night for the first time I ventured down an area of back to back houses in a rather poor district. At the end of the street, I saw a brick walled tunnel, the width of a car and about twenty five yards long. Being a believer in not shining a torch unless necessary, I entered the tunnel in the darkness and halfway along stepped into a water filled pothole. The puddle wasn't quite deep enough to reach the top of my boots, but the bottoms of my trousers were wet through so I turned back. I was twenty yards down the street when I heard a sash window being opened and immediately a jet of urine came from the open window and splashed onto the road about five yards ahead. I never went down that street again, nor did I ever know what was at the end of the tunnel.

In the fourteen months at Walton I met two sailors that I knew. The crew of HMS Cooke were mostly from the Liverpool area. I was walking along Westminster Road when across the road I saw one of the stokers with another man. I started to cross the road to them when the stoker recognised me. The other man however quickly ran away. When I asked why the man had run off, I was told that he thought I might have been after him...

The second meeting with an old crew member was more remarkable. It was Grand National day and I was on point duty at Aintree where the road from Bootle met the very busy A59 from Liverpool. Trams were appearing one after another from Liverpool. I stopped the traffic from Liverpool, the first of which was a tram; then I turned around to let the Bootle traffic filter left to Aintree. As the cars moved to turn left, I realised that a man and a woman had joined me in the centre of the road. It was Dick Thomas, one of the three men who had become my friends on the first day in the Royal Navy. The lady was his wife. I can't imagine what all the people thought seeing a policeman and two civilians in a clinch together in the middle of a busy junction. I asked them to go back to the footpath until I could clear the traffic from Liverpool which was now stretching out of sight. After the war, Dick had gone back to his job as a railway telegraphist at Crewe and married. He and his wife had decided to visit the Grand National that day and had been sitting at the front of the tram which I had stopped.

Dick was surprised to see me as he hadn't known I had become a policeman, and said to his wife, "That's Jack Wilson", and then quickly jumped off the tram. We had a lovely chat after I had restored the traffic situation, and my parting words to him were, "perhaps we will be able to meet again", but it was thirty or so years later when we eventually met up again. I was then working for Boots the chemist and had an enquiry in Crewe. I knew that Dick had gone back to his original job, but by now would have retired, so I went to the railway station to see if I could find out his address. When I explained the reason for my request, the man in the communications department gave me his address in Crewe. He also gave me the sad news that Dick had terminal cancer and was a very poorly man.

I had gone to find him with the idea that the four friends might have had a get-together, but that hope was now shattered. Dick opened the door and was just as surprised as I had been in Liverpool. His wife was with him and we all chatted away for several hours during which time I had a meal with them. He was bright and cheery, but I am certain that he realised that I knew of his illness. I had a very miserable journey home to Heywood and sadly Dick died within six months.

I always seemed too busy to bother with minor

offences, but one such incident seems to stick in my mind. There was a small park with a very well used footpath which had the sign, 'Cycling not allowed' with the usual Bye Law information. Hundreds of pedestrians used the path to and from work, but although most cycles had a bell, people constantly had to step aside. I thought I could rectify this so one morning I waited at one end and booked the first few cyclists fully expecting them to get an official caution. Instead they were summoned to appear at the magistrate's court. Then I really did get a surprise, as I was handed the summons personally to serve it on the one man who lived in Walton. I knocked on his door with the document in my hand, and his first few words were, "come in officer." I entered and his wife said, "Would you like a cup of tea?" I felt as though I was the guilty person!

Thereafter, I used to give people my own caution to minor offences and none ever let me down. With the River Mersey as its boundary, one of the nice things about the City Force was that anyone who couldn't swim was taught to. For two hours each week I went to one of the City public baths where we had our own instructor; but also with us was a group of disabled ex-soldiers and some small children, some with no arms or legs. It gave me the impetus to persevere and so six weeks later I passed my life saving test.

I have left many other little snippets out and this is just a selection of the events which happened in one year out of the thirty one I served as a policeman. I enjoyed my new job and felt that I was in a wonderful position to help people, and although the weekly wage of £5 was good, Nan and I found it almost impossible to keep our heads above water living apart. Out of the class of twelve at the training school, only four of us were left.

I enquired if I was any nearer to getting a police house and the answer was negative. Nan and I discussed our situation. I knew that the Lancashire force would accept me and there was the possibility that I would be able to work in a town closer to Clitheroe. I earlier mentioned the

Deputy Chief Constable, and it was to him that I turned. The City Force was still under staffed so it wasn't going to be easy, and no-one had ever been transferred. I explained my situation to him, about Nan and my son living in Clitheroe in our own house whilst I was still lodging at Kirby Hostel. I explained that if it was not possible for me to get a transfer to the Lancashire Constabulary, I would have to resign from Liverpool City Police. Mr Martin was an extremely nice gentleman and he realised what would happen to the Force if I was allowed to transfer. However, he did decide to sanction my transfer which was arranged straight away. I was very grateful and told him that I would never forget him or his kindness. A year later I saw him again when I played for the Lancashire Constabulary football team against Liverpool at Liverpool and they thumped us 5:2.

I handed in my uniform and accessories and said goodbye especially to the Station Sergeant at Walton. None of them wanted me to leave but their good wishes were nice as I left the City to go to an entirely different environment in Lancashire; from busy city to sleepy market town.

Police Constable, Clitheroe 1947-1958

At Lancashire Constabulary headquarters Hutton, I was accepted into the Force as Constable 1520 and wondered where I would be stationed. I was delighted to find that I would start in my own town of Clitheroe. I understood that it was the first time that this had happened.

During my teenage years, Clitheroe had been the smallest Borough Force in the Country. Chief Constable Thomson had been an Inspector in Lancashire. The sergeant there was Whitehead and there were twelve constables and a detective constable. By 1946, Clitheroe Borough Police was amalgamated into the Lancashire Constabulary as a section of Accrington. Seven of the policemen were still serving. Sergeant Whitehead had become Inspector and there were three sergeants. Clitheroe is a small market town with a Norman castle nestling in the Ribble Valley under the shadow of Pendle Hill with a population of around 13,000. Before the police amalgamation, the villages of Whalley, Pendleton, Chatburn and Downham were outside the Borough, but were now included in the Clitheroe section. These four villages were under the control of Sergeant Turner who resided in Whalley Police Station. The Borough boundary on the North and West was the River Ribble and the West Riding of Yorkshire was beyond. The top of Pendle Hill was on the eastern side, Nelson division on the other side and south of Whalley was Blackburn Division.

When I left the Royal Navy, Nan didn't work anymore and we struggled until I was transferred to Clitheroe. Our home at 1 Mitchell St was a three up, three down terraced house without a bathroom. The front faced onto a coal yard and the railway line which ran from Blackburn to Hellifield and ultimately to Carlisle. There was a side door which we used instead of a front door and also a door into the small back yard and the water closet. The biggest item in the yard was a tin bath hanging on the wall. On two out of three weeks Nan and I used it, but on the third week when I was on nights, only she got the benefit. The bath needed quite a few buckets full of hot water from the geyser in the kitchen, but was quite cosy in front of a roaring fire. Our front parlour was bare and we never did use it.

When I left my house to walk to the Police Station about a mile away, I wondered what differences I might find between a large city and a small town like Clitheroe. Having dealt with the city, I thought that at least Clitheroe must be easier. How wrong I was.

At 9am, Phyllis the office clerk took me into the back room and Sergeant Sutcliffe came out of the sergeant's office to meet me. In the middle of what was the parade room was a large billiard table no longer used for the sport, which had a wooden top. It served as a worktable and also a dining table. There was a roaring coal fire, but no comfortable chairs. Two typewriters were available. Phyllis offered to teach me to type and I accepted her offer but never improved any further than two finger typing. The station was open to the public from 6am to 10pm, but through the night was only open at the end of each hour. Duties were now 6am-2pm; 2pm-10pm and the night shift 10pm-6am. However, subject to the men available, there were two other shifts; 10am-6pm and 6pm-2am. It was quite common for one constable to be on duty between 2am and 6am. The nearest policeman to him was eight miles away in Lancashire and eighteen miles away in Yorkshire.

Parading on duty was similar to Liverpool: stand in line, baton between two hands with handcuffs and whistle chain overhanging the baton. Pocket books were also examined to ensure every word was in ink. The sergeant read out anything of importance, including stolen cars whose registration numbers had to be written in our pocket books, and then he would tell us which of the two beats we would occupy. Number one beat covered the town centre, and number two beat, the outskirts. He would indicate the hourly points (no tram lines here), so if he wanted you, he had to be there. The sergeant would have a car available to him, but for us number two beat was a cycle beat. A police cycle was available, but if you had your own cycle, it was worth 6d a day so I bought a new bike.

I was allocated for duty with Halliwell and Buchanan. The rest of the first day was spent with all the different ledgers including Lost and Found Property which would be itemised and numbered, and the Licensed Premises Book recording all visits to pubs. One book for the sergeants recorded the times of each visit to a constable. All of this was very different to the City Force. Having a large and very busy cattle market, I was obliged very quickly to swat up on the numerous Diseases of Animals Regulations and familiarise myself with all the documents and licenses required by the farmers who came in daily.

Knowledge of the exact movements of cattle was essential if an outbreak occurred. Within a few weeks, I was one of only a few constables to be made Diseases of Animals Inspectors and during my time in Clitheroe I dealt with Foot and Mouth, Foul Pest, Swine Fever and most dangerous of all, Anthrax. I was the youngest Diseases of Animals Inspector, but I was also the youngest of the policeman in Clitheroe until I was joined by John Burnett and Gordon Walsh also natives of Clitheroe; and another friend of mine, Dick Sagar who joined Lancashire County and went to Accrington.

Clitheroe Police Station was a very old stone building which today is a warm building with lovely working conditions. However, then it was a cold building even though water pipes ran in all directions from a coke boiler in the cellar. The number one beat bobby had to perform an unusual task which in all possibility no other bobby in the county had to perform. He had to clean out the fire in the parade room and replenish the very large coal scuttle, then go down to the boiler room, rake out all the cinders and ash and transfer them to the dustbin in the back yard. Then it would be office duty until 7am.

During the night shift after refreshments, I would occasionally look through old records which went a long way back, and I was amazed at what people were getting arrested for: stealing apples and even one case of stealing a penny bun from a market stall. One year in the eighteen hundreds, the total stolen in a year was the grand sum of £26.

I was very proud to be in my own town and I wanted to look after its residents. I am a firm believer in policemen residing in the town where they work, because if you do, you want it to be a safe place to live in. In Liverpool I had worked my shift, and then forgotten about duty until the next day; but now I was looking at things in a different light, realising that you were never really off duty. My home became similar to a village police station, so when I was out my wife took any messages. I was so well known that most people passed the time of day with me and I gave a little salute to all the elderly ladies I knew. This seemed to give them a lot of pleasure. Several of the pre-war policemen were still serving.

Ken Halliwell was my working companion for a few years. Having been a Coldstream Guardsman, he used to recount his wartime stories, but he had also been on sentry duty at Buckingham Palace, and his stories of what happened there remain with me. Sadly, Ken got cancer in his left eye which was eventually removed and replaced with a glass one, but the cancer had spread and this ultimately robbed him of his life. The loss of his eye somewhat handicapped him in our numerous encounters with the three hundred Irish navvies who worked on the Manchester water pipe which passed through the Ribble Valley. We all walked in escort when his Union draped coffin was slowly conveyed from his home to Clitheroe Cemetery. Many of the stories I can remember took place in Ken's company, but I will recount them later.

For a small section of such a large County Force there was considerable movement in the ranks. On my arrival, as well as the ex-borough men, were five other ex-army recruits: Knight, Morris, Buchanan, Grimshaw and Waller. Knight had realised how busy the railway station was and established a successful taxi service. Morris became the licensee of a hotel in the town centre. Of the other three, two were requested to resign and one was sent to prison. I was soon to become a water bailiff: unique in the Force.

Salmon Poaching

Many of the Borough and County Court magistrates were large land owners. Three of these were Lord Clitheroe, Lady Hornby and Lady Aspinall. The River Ribble which separated the two counties was, and still is a renowned salmon and trout river, but it was also the hunting grounds for four poachers, a father, two sons and a nephew who were nick-named 'The Donnicks'. Their motto was, 'Fish are born free.' Of course, fishing in a river requires a licence plus a permit to fish on private land. River banks were private, so the land owners employed water bailiffs, often ex-village Bobbies and there were several patrolling the Ribble Valley. The gang would reconnoitre which deep pools held salmon, then late in the evening two would wade or swim across the water each holding the end of a large net. The four would then close in trapping all the fish between the two nets. The wardens, having tried unsuccessfully to catch them were at their wit's end and so was Sergeant Sutcliffe. It was known how fast I could move, so I was made a bailiff. I knew these men who were also hen thieves.

I was aware of their meeting place in Henthorne Park. There were benches in the park with a very thick privet fence behind. I used to listen to them from behind that fence and wonder what would have happened if they had seen me. One evening, I heard them talking about going to Sawley, probably on the next evening, and this was just beyond the Borough boundary. The bailiffs turned out along with Sergeant Sutcliffe and me and we waited quietly out of sight. They arrived, caught two large salmon in the nets and when they had finished we pounced. Three of them escaped, but I caught one of the sons. All four of the gang were eventually caught red handed and the magistrate gave them a hefty fine and a severe warning never to poach again.

Every cloud has a silver lining as they say, because the bailiffs gave the fish out to be shared amongst the police officers back at the station. The nets were taken back to the police station and stored in a little-used cell to dry out and for the bailiffs to collect later. One morning the Inspector approached me and asked me if I knew anything about the nets in the cell. I asked him why and he informed me that they were soaking wet. I had seen them the day before and they were dry. It appears that the two night duty constables had either let the poachers use the nets or had used them themselves. Both constables were married but were never on the same shift as me. I was aware however, that when there was no duty sergeant they were using two of the cells for 'one night stands'. Both constables resigned from the force and moved away from the town.

Inspector Whitehead and Sergeant Cutler both retired and Sergeant Robinson also had to leave the force. I never really knew the reason, but he went A.W.O.L. (Absent without Office of Leave) and it would seem that he was in London instead of policing in Clitheroe. He returned home and I was told to bring him in. The actual words used were, "arrest him!" I didn't. Instead, we walked together to the police station. He was a delightful chap who had risen to the rank of Captain in the war, and he suddenly flipped which brought about his dismissal from the police. I just hoped that he received his full pension, but never saw him again.

Three local lads then joined the police force: John Burnett, Richard Sagar, son of the Borough PC Sagar and Gordon Walsh. After completing their training, Walsh and Burnett served for a short period in Clitheroe before transferring to other towns.

Murder

At 7am, Maud Taylor the police station cleaner arrived for her two hour cleaning shift. She was middle aged and she and her husband, a bus inspector, knew me from my very early life as both families attended St James Church. They were a lovely couple. One day she didn't turn up for work and so someone went round to her home which was ¼ mile away and found that she had been strangled. Clifford, her husband had become insane during the night and he had killed her. The Police surgeon certified him and he was charged with her murder. Eventually he was taken to a secure mental hospital where he died. It was a sad police station for some considerable time because everyone had liked her.

It was around this point in my career that I started to keep newspaper cuttings regarding the incidents that I had played a part in. I was in fact, apprehending more people than D.C. Crabtree. Some of these incidents are worth a separate mention, but there were many others whose headlines read as follows:

Tyre theft from works
13year old girl stole gold wrist watch
11year old boy sent to approved school
Boys admitting breaking into bakery sent to approved school
Joy rides send boys to court
Clitheroe sailor joy rides on stolen cars
Couple steal from Old Folks Club
Dog lover stole Alsatian
Former Italian policeman had missing tarpaulin
Court hears of a £59 stolen car
3 months hard labour for stealing taps

In the 1940's and 50's and long before that, policemen used to ensure that children going to and from school got safely across the busy A59 main road. If we were unable to get to the schools, the head teacher would be informed and a teacher would take on this duty. I can imagine what teachers would say today if this was asked of them!

Theft from Nursery

One Monday I was on the outer beat cycling down Edisford Road, when I saw Ken, a school friend of mine tending his garden. I stopped to have a little chat with him. By trade, he was a landscape gardener and always had a beautiful display in his front garden. Whilst admiring his plants, I noticed about fifteen miniature shrubs; varieties which I had never seen and he told me that they were new. What a good idea I thought, planting something that would draw attention to his trade, then off I went.

The following day I read the message pad as usual and there was a message from the owner of a Nursery in Barrow, two miles away informing us that fifteen miniature shrubs had been stolen over the weekend. I told Phyllis that I knew where the shrubs were and would be back in half an hour. Ken was in so I asked him to dig up a couple of the shrubs as we were going to the police station with them. I told him that I knew where they had come from so he pleaded guilty to theft and the Nursery got all their shrubs back. It wasn't a pleasant job, arresting a friend, but I always knew that if I let someone off for theft then it would put me in an awful position if the next criminal that was arrested and charged found out. If someone higher up than me made the decision to caution, then it was fine.

Advertiser headline: 'Ribble bus driver fired!'

A telephone message had been received about a failure to stop on the A59 at Salmesbury, about eight miles from Clitheroe. A bus heading north, had for no apparent reason swerved and collided with a coach heading in the opposite direction and then failed to stop. There were only scratches and minor damage plus a broken mirror to the coach, but glass thought to be from the offside mirror of the bus was in the roadway. Sergeant Sutcliffe told me to stop all buses so that we could examine their mirrors. Several buses stopped, all with mirrors intact, then the Preston to Clitheroe bus arrived with only one mile to go to the bus depot and he too seemed to have his mirror intact. It was then that I noticed the glitter of glass on the driver's knees. When I asked him to wind his window up, there was no glass, the majority of it being under his feet. He was sacked and later fined for failure to stop.

Shoe theft

A little intuition came in handy when a shoe shop had a

costly pair of boots stolen from the doorway of the shop where they had been hanging on display with other footwear. On the floor was a newspaper in which had been chips, so I went to the nearest fish and chip shop which was about half a mile away and found out that two Scotsmen had been in for a takeaway and they were reputedly seen heading for the railway station. This was my next port of call. The porter said that a man had caught the Preston train with the boots hanging round his neck, so I made a telephone call to the railway police who nabbed him on the North bound platform in Preston. I went on the next train and collected him. The newspaper cutting read: '*Theft of shoes. Smart capture at Preston Station*'. The defendant had just come out of prison for housebreaking and was given the choice of a fine or one month in jail. He paid the fine.

By July in 1948, I had been in the Section for a year and seemed to be getting a lot of little interesting jobs to deal with. The local bookmaker was complaining about an illegal betting shop. Now, I have never been on the side of the bookmaker as there is only ever one winner and that is the bookmaker. There are no poor bookmakers, however in this case the bookmaker was justified in his grumblings. The premises used for the illegal shop was a blacksmith's and in the next three days at lunchtime, I kept observation from the front garden of a large house fifty yards away. Not one animal entered the smithy, but 110 men and women did. A warrant was obtained and on the following day lead by Inspector Whitehead, Sergeant Sutcliffe and three constables, we raided the smithy. There were thirteen customers who of course gave some varied replies when asked for their purpose in being at the smithy, the best one being, "I've come in to book a coach trip to Harrogate". They were all arrested and a couple of weeks later fined.

Every ten years, Clitheroe has a torchlight procession with over 100 floats. In 1948, one month after the raid, I was on duty when alongside me appeared a lorry carrying a placard which pronounced: 'Local Smithy. No horses allowed. Four to one bar one.' This, together with a photograph appeared in the local newspaper the following week. The newspaper caption read: '*Some Smithy! Wittiest of all, at least to those in the know, was a tableau depicting a Smithy, but not the sort that stood beneath the spreading chestnut tree. The only horses about the place had familiar names.*'

Press cuttings circa 1949

'*Boy took biscuits from a market stall*' – He ate about 9lbs worth, then stole a pedal cycle.

'*Stole lanterns from ministry store*' - An eleven year old boy was out of parental control and for taking younger children with him, was sent to an approved school.

'*Man and woman charged*' - eleven year old used as a tool for Clitheroe thefts. A tiny boy was used and pushed through very small windows in various shops to facilitate their entry into the premises.

'*Let sleeping stones lie*' – Damage to two ornamental stone gryphons in Clitheroe Castle.

'*An eye for an eye*' – Man arrested for stealing a pet rabbit. He said he had had one pinched.

On Bank holidays, Clitheroe would burst at the seams with day trippers in their thousands appearing on the trains and the numerous buses. Two of the most popular villages in the North West were within three miles; Waddington just across the river in Yorkshire and Downham of the Pendle Witches fame, which was three miles to the north. More than five hundred coaches from Yorkshire also traversed the A59 en route to Blackpool. I used to spend a lot of time at the main Ribble bus terminus close to Clitheroe Royal Grammar School, usually assisting lost souls who wanted to catch local village buses which had a separate terminus outside the railway station ¼ mile away. On Bank Holiday evenings, traffic would be nose to tail going south as far as Whalley, four miles away.

Bomb incident

During the war, the Royal Engineers who were based in Low Moor Mill used a patch of moorland on Pendle Hill as a training ground for the firing of trench mortar, smoke or high explosive bombs. I had commenced the 2pm-10pm shift and was standing in the market place one Sunday afternoon thinking about how nice it would be to take my family for a walk when Jim Crabtree, now a sergeant came racing up to me in the police car.

"Jump in quick," he urged. "A bomb has exploded on Pendle Hill!"

Derek Shaw, a twenty year old soldier on leave, together with two younger friends had gone walking on the fells. They had taken a terrier with the intention of catching rabbits and were alongside one of the many stone walls when Derek had spotted the fins of a mortar bomb sticking up from the ground. The bomb was of course rusty and many years old, but to frighten the lads, he said, "If I touch this against the wall it will explode." He did just that, believing it was just a smoke bomb. In reality it was highly explosive, so as the nose of the bomb touched the wall, it exploded. The soldier's right arm was blown off up to the elbow, but his sixteen year old friend had moved behind him and taken a lot of shrapnel wounds. The other boy, a fourteen year old, was not so lucky and was killed instantly. The soldier then tried to run back down the hillside, but after a hundred yards collapsed. Two male hikers going up the hill, one of whom was proficient in first aid stayed with him. The son of a local farmer heard the explosion, saw the smoke rising in the air and the sheep scattering on the hillside, so he ran the half a mile towards the spot, then ran a further mile to the nearest telephone which allowed the police and ambulance to receive the call.

As we neared the scene we were followed by an ambulance, but the nearest access point was along a rough farm track and into the farm yard still ¼ of a mile away. A stretcher was taken up the very rough terrain to Derek Shaw who was by this time suffering from a severe loss of blood. We carried him down to the waiting ambulance and he was taken the ten miles to Blackburn Infirmary. A second ambulance appeared so we once again crossed the undulating rough ground to the badly injured boy who was being tended to by the two hikers. He too was carried down to the ambulance and then taken off to Blackburn Infirmary. The first ambulance driver had been asked to ring the police to arrange for a coffin to be brought up for the boy who had died and so began our third trip up. The little terrier had stayed by this boy's side from the moment he had died.

The hikers and the farmer's son had done an excellent job in helping the two injured men. That same evening, the dead boy was taken to the mortuary and the police surgeon did the post mortem with me present.

On the Monday morning, I caught the bus into Blackburn and went to interview the soldier at Blackburn Infirmary where he was sitting up in bed and just about to strike a match on his bandaged stump so that he could smoke a cigarette. He told me what he had done and sadly that night he also died from shock. The sixteen year old who had suffered multiple shrapnel injuries recovered. The Royal Engineers sent a large squad of soldiers to sweep the area in close formation and they found a second unexploded bomb. Apparently, over time it is possible for metal objects to come up to the surface after they have been previously buried. For a long time afterwards, notices warning hikers of the possible dangers were placed in the area.

Wellsprings Hotel

The Wellsprings Hotel is situated at the top of Pendle Hill on the only road from Clitheroe to Sabden village and creates the Eastern boundary of Clitheroe Borough. My sergeant at that time was called Sutcliffe, who was a pre-war officer obsessed with the out of hours drinking that was going on way into the early hours of the morning at weekends. We knew it was taking place because we could see the lights of the pub on the hill three miles away. We had attempted on numerous occasions to put a stop to it, but on each occasion the pub would be full of people with not a drink in sight. We suspected that our detective constable was the informant. He was always known to be a bit of a ladies man, and was a frequent patron of the pub.

On one occasion I reported for duty at 10 am having gone off duty at 2am earlier in the morning and the Inspector asked me if I had been visited by the Sergeant during the previous night. I informed him that he'd visited me at 10:15pm and that I had seen him again when I went off duty. He informed me that a friend of his had been in the Wellsprings Pub at 11 pm and had seen him washing pots in the kitchen and shortly after was seen leaving in the direction of Sabden with the barmaid. I'm not aware if anything was ever said to the sergeant but it did remind me of all the times we had tried unsuccessfully to raid the pub for after-hours drinking.

After I retired I visited Sutcliffe who had retired as a Chief Inspector in Hyde some years previously and gone to Cheshire on his retirement. He told me why we had never been able to catch the Wellsprings Hotel out. Evidently the licensee had rigged up the cattle grid half a mile from the hotel with a wire that ran up to the inn. They also knew when the sergeant and I were on duty together and were on the lookout for us. When a vehicle crossed the grid the vibrations travelled along the wire and the manager was forewarned with enough time to get the drinks cleared away.

Fire!

A newspaper headline informed the readers; *'Brothers help to fight fire'* – My brother Cecil was just about to enter my home when he saw a house garage on fire. He shouted and I joined him and together with the house owner, also named Wilson, we were able to save a motor car and two motor cycles from the blazing garage; a good effort for three Wilsons!

I have been to some very large fires in my time, but the most gruesome was a house fire in the Henthorne district. An elderly disabled man was smoking whilst sitting in front of a coal fire. The fire brigade were called to deal with the house fire but before it was extinguished the downstairs was gutted. The fire chief came to the conclusion that the old man had dropped the cigarette and in trying to retrieve it had fallen forward and into the fire. He must have died a terrible death, with a hundred percent burns leaving his face completely unrecognisable. The post mortem was dreadful.

Clive

In January 1950, Clive was born in 1 Mitchell St, and Ray who was five at this time, was attending St James school. Within a few weeks, Clive was losing weight instead of gaining and had become very ill. At three months old, the local doctor decided that the problem was most likely a blocked valve in his stomach and he was taken to Accrington hospital where there was a children's ward. An operation was immediately performed and for several nights Nan and I stayed at the hospital. Nan and I were church goers from the day we had been born and it was our faith which kept us going throughout that difficult time. After five days our little baby boy smiled and we knew he would be safe. We were able to take him back home and the hospital surgeon told us to get as much Nestles condensed milk as possible as it was his only cure at that time, but condensed milk was rationed in those days. From the day I had been born, the family grocers were Jim and Amy Brewer who still had the corner shop thirty yards from us and they were treasures. They asked the locals to give up their ration tickets to allow us to obtain enough milk for Clive to recover, and they did. Throughout our lives we would remember those days and even now when I pass Accrington hospital with Clive en-route to a football ground, I whisper, 'Thank you God'.

Promotion

After two years, it was possible to take the sergeants educational exam which consisted of maths, English and a general knowledge paper, which I passed. After four years, I was able to take the police duties exam. There were three papers in all, a traffic, crime and general paper which I also passed. It was also possible after four years to take the Inspectors educational exam, a little stiffer in content but still three papers; maths, English and general knowledge. I also passed these exams. It was then in the 1950's that it was almost a case of 'waiting for dead men's shoes', until the divisional Superintendent recommended you for your appointment to sergeant. Two men whom I knew who were well known in County HQ received their stripes after six years of service and it created a great disturbance with men who had a lot of service, but both were good policemen and each eventually gained Chief Superintendent Status. After ten years in the service in Lancashire, I finally became sergeant.

There was a period of about six months when the detective at Clitheroe was seconded to the Met police in London to assist with the application and interviewing of people wanting to become British citizens and so I was appointed Detective in his absence. I won't describe the number of cases I dealt with but when he returned, my detection rate was 90 percent. Jim did make a very interesting comment to me on his return from London. He said that he had made a lot of money from his enquiries. I took this to be what is commonly known as 'back-handers'.

'Prison for Bestial conduct'

Another sad incident resulted in the arrest of a lorry driver from Manchester who indecently assaulted two little sisters, one aged eight and the other five. The incident happened in Whalley, when the driver stopped and told the children he would take them home. He eventually dropped them off before reaching their home, but the eight year old told her mother and I was detailed to deal with it. I interviewed a lot of people and although he pleaded 'not guilty', he was sent to prison for twelve months.

Clitheroe street fight… two sent to prison

It was a Friday evening and the usual bus-loads of Irish navvies were in town. Two were fighting so I told them it was time for them to return to camp. Two hours later, they were still fighting, but now with others. PC Halliwell joined me and we picked out the two large men, and as Halliwell only had one eye, I chose the larger of the two drunks. He struck out and gave me an almighty blow in my chest, and consequently I needed physiotherapy occasionally for the next ten years. We eventually dragged them to the police station a hundred yards away, and I do confess that a certain part of his anatomy collided with the cell door on his way in! I could have charged him with assault, but drunks never know much about their antics the morning after. The Mayor, Councillor Rushton had said," We cannot have the town disturbed in this manner and we feel that unless something more drastic than a fine is imposed, this sort of thing will continue." They went to prison for a month.

Miners Outing Buck Inn

Saturday nights in Clitheroe could often be violent and so instead of two constables on separate beats, there was a tendency to stay together until the dance hall emptied and the buses stopped running. My shift partner for the whole time until he died of eye cancer was Ken Halliwell. He had been a young policeman before the war and served in the Coldstream guards before returning to duty after the war. One Saturday night I went into the police station and took a call from the licensee at the Buck Inn. He informed me that a coach full of miners from Wigan had been drinking for several hours, including the driver, and when he had called time he overheard one of them suggest that they should go to the pub on the top of Pendle Hill and he watched as the coach set off along Pendle Road.

I knew Ken was in the Market Place so I went to him and together we walked up to the Buck Inn. The pub was closed and because it had been raining earlier in the evening, the road was wet in places and being summertime and lighter evenings, we could follow the coach tracks. What happened next would not have occurred had the coach followed the straight road to the Wellsprings Inn. However after 100 yards it had turned left into a street which became a cul-de-sac after ¾ of a mile. We continued to follow the wheel tracks and the street became narrower until eventually there were no more houses. On one side was a mill and on the other was a small stream which turned the water wheel on the mill. There was no sign of the coach so we continued to walk a further 300 yards until the tarmac stopped. Turning sharp right there was a farm track leading uphill. By now it was pitch black but ahead of us we could hear raised voices. The people shouting and swearing and coming towards us in twos and threes were drunken miners. None of them were actually on the farm track and I suspect that none of them saw us.

We continued to walk along the path and presently we came across the coach lying on its side. Alongside it was the driver, who was clearly worse for wear and under the influence of alcohol so I cautioned him and put him under arrest. It was clear that the coach must have been moving very slowly as there was no damage to the vehicle and none of the passengers were injured.

Of course we had to walk the driver back to the police station which was pretty slow going. When we were about 200 yards away from the station, the driver who was now walking perfectly normally and speaking clearly, asked if we were arresting him for drunk driving. I informed him that we would not be doing that; but instead we were taking him back to the police station where he could phone his boss and explain to him what he had done to the coach.

Had we arrested him we would have had to find the sergeant to listen to his story, then we'd have had to call out the police doctor to carry out the blood tests. In those days the limit was much higher than today and he would probably have shown that he was capable of driving. No one was injured and no damage was caused to anyone else's property.

Looking back a number of things strike me:

When the coach went over it must have been absolute chaos; many of the miners were probably asleep, the rest in a drunken stupor and yet no one was injured. There was complete darkness in the field except for the coach headlights which were directed up the hill. They must have seen the lights of the town in the distance and set off walking towards the lights. When they reached the town, there were no buses or trains running so how they got back to Wigan is a puzzle and for the rest of our shift neither Ken nor I saw any sign of any of the miners, although I spent quite some time typing up my occurrence report.

Shop breaking 24 Well Terrace

Several times over a period of weeks I noticed an old lady, aged about 75, coming to the Police Station to report that her small shop was frequently being broken into but no one was doing anything about it. I went to see her and found that her kitchen window opened into the back yard and the transom part was boarded up on the outside. She told me she went for a walk between 12 noon and 1pm every day, and although everything looked secure, several packs of cigarettes were missing.

I told her to go for her usual walk that day and I would watch her home. There was a back street which was open at both ends and her shop was in the middle of twenty houses. I noticed that the opposite side of the back street was also the rear wall of a fruit and vegetable warehouse which had windows overlooking the whole of the street, so by standing on a ladder I could watch the rear of her shop through a window. At 12 o'clock, a 17 year old youth appeared at the bottom of the street, but he had only walked about twenty yards when a lady from one of the other houses came out to hang out her washing and the youth carried on walking to the top and disappeared.

Ten minutes later he came back from the bottom end and this time two children came out of another gate and started to play football and the youth once again carried on walking to the top of the street and disappeared. I started to worry that the shop owner would return and prevent the youth from doing whatever it was he was up to so I arranged for the lady to be intercepted and continued to watch. At 12.50 the youth returned and this time he jumped over the wall and prised off the board over the window, entering the house through the window.

I rushed around to the rear of the house to wait for him to come out. Unfortunately he was able to see the top of my helmet over the wall and he climbed onto the roof of the kitchen and then jumped from one kitchen roof to another down to the end of the street. I followed him along the back. The youth was known to me and was arrested. At court he pleaded guilty to a number of other counts of theft from 24 Well Terrace for which he received a prison sentence.

Waddington Constable Loses Prisoner

One thing I always did, whatever my rank, was to read the telephone message pad from the previous day. I came on duty at 10 pm for night duty and I read a brief account of a Waddington Policeman losing a prisoner.

It would appear that at about 5pm the policeman was in his car watching traffic on the narrow country road from the Trough of Bowland to Whalley. He stopped a car heading south with two male occupants, the driver being a white Caucasian and his passenger of Afro Caribbean descent. The police officer opened the boot and discovered that it was full of cigarettes and cigars, clearly the proceeds from a theft somewhere. It was a dark winter's evening and the constable confiscated the car keys and then escorted the two men to a nearby public house. Unfortunately as they were entering the pub, the driver went in first, ahead of the constable who in turn was being followed by the passenger; only he wasn't. When the policeman turned around the passenger had disappeared into the night. Having read the account I went out on patrol.

At 1 am I returned to the police station for the half hour night break and whilst there, a phone call came through from the GPO phone operator in Clitheroe saying that he had taken a call from a telephone box at Rimmington from a man with a peculiar accent who needed help getting a taxi. Rimmington is six miles north of Clitheroe and three miles into the West Riding Police area. It occurred to me that this could be the missing prisoner even though it was ten miles from the public house. I phoned the Divisional Headquarters and asked if a car could pick me up to investigate. The driver was known to me and I told him to take the A59 to Chatburn, then on to Downham and eventually Rimmington. We didn't have the blue lights flashing. As we were travelling along the road we saw a vehicle approaching us in the opposite direction and it became apparent that we would be unable to pass each other in a dip in the narrow road. We both stopped about twenty yards apart and sitting in the car was a dark skinned man who realised that we were in a police car. He jumped out, leaped over a wall and into the darkness. I also jumped out and over the wall which turned out to be a twelve foot drop into a rocky stream, but fortunately I landed on both feet. I found myself in a wooded area with no moonlight, listening to the sound of running water whilst looking for a dark skinned man! I used my torch to look in all directions but soon realised it was going to be futile and after ten minutes I gave up the search.

I reported my account to the early duty men at 6 am, and at 8am a train driver travelling between Chatburn and Clitheroe reported seeing a dark skinned man walking alongside the railway line. He was picked up and handed over to West Riding Police. Looking back I realised that I had been quite lucky because the drop on the other side of the wall could have been much further that the twelve feet. Perhaps the proverb 'Look before you leap,' was first phrased in a similar situation!

Near Miss!

Ken Halliwell and I were together one late night in Whalley Road, both holding our cycles, when we saw a car approaching from the town centre. It was veering all over the road. I gave Ken my cycle and held my hand up for the driver to stop from a reasonable safe distance, but he drove past. There was a car behind the drunk which stopped so I got in and I asked the driver to follow the car ahead. We followed it for three miles trying unsuccessfully to get ahead of it, but finally managing to overtake it just before Whalley centre. I alighted and stood in the centre of the road with my hand up, but he came straight for me and at the last second I had just enough time to jump aside. However, he did stop about twenty yards beyond me and I grabbed him before he had time to set off again. I thanked my 'good shepherd' as he waited by the roadside to see if I needed him again. At Whalley police station the erratic driver was charged with drunk driving. A second man also inside the car who was the owner of the vehicle was also charged with several aiding and abetting offences.

Trips out with the police

During my years in Clitheroe, I went on duty several times to Aintree Racecourse on Grand National Day. It was always a welcome day out. On my first visit I was on the level ground at the final jump before the run-in to the finishing line. There were so many people between me and the race track that all I saw were the heads of the jockeys and the horses ears as they topped the jump. My next visit to Aintree provided me with a better position to see the races from the bottom step of the Enclosure stand, but once again there were thousands of people in front of me. On the third and last visit I made there, I was posted right against the first fence. It was like the Charge of the Light Brigade; the thundering hooves shook the ground and the whole lot went over en-bloc. Two horses fell but there were no injuries. This final visit was by far the best as the well-off were drinking champagne and devouring beautiful sandwiches which they shared with us.

My favourite outing was in 1953 when I was one of the few constables from each division to go to London for three days to the coronation of Queen Elizabeth the second. We were billeted in tents in Hyde Park and I had a boat trip on the River Thames, visited the Tower and one evening went to a stage show at the London Palladium Theatre. Jimmy Edwards, Vera Lynn and Tony Hancock were the star performers – great stuff!

Our contingent was on duty on Oxford Street on the edge of the pavement and the whole procession passed by. The spectators and the shops shared out their goodies and it certainly was a day to remember. Twenty five years later I was one of the two officers in each division to receive the Queen's Silver Jubilee medal.

By this time all the Borough police had departed. Sergeant Sutcliffe was the last, having been promoted to Inspector and gone to Hyde. Sergeants Andrews and Ashcroft soon arrived closely followed by Jim Crabtree, and Chief Inspector Fairclough was in charge.

The 'Cold War' with Russia was on everyone's mind making civil defence essential. I was given the task of finding four defence wardens and as all my former Infant and Junior School teachers were still teaching, I invited them to become involved and they all agreed. They were defence wardens in name only as thankfully, they were never needed.

Another assignment and an annual event, was to check and see if all the dog owners had their dog licenses. This was three day's work as I always gave them two days to get a license so no-one was ever booked.

Animal cases

Sergeant Ashcroft came to Clitheroe from Garstang, which like Clitheroe had a large cattle market. He was the most knowledgeable policeman in Lancashire about animal diseases and the Law and Order offences connected with the haulage of livestock. He realised that I was interested and so I became his pupil. He had a Cocker Spaniel which he took with him on duty from 6am till 8am and after midnight on night duty and so I often went walkies with them. I learned everything he knew. One of the things he was very strict about was the cleaning of the cattle lorries. They were not being swilled out between loads, but under my influence, they did. I reported many of the drivers and they were fined at the Magistrates Court. The farmers appreciated what I was doing, but the cattle dealers didn't like me and they always knew when I was on duty. It was whilst I was stopping lorries on the A59 that I was able to report a horse dealer for cruelty. I discovered that six horses in a horse box had been tethered nose to tail instead of nose to nose. This meant that the front row of three had been kicking the three behind them causing injury. Had there been a gate between each row of three, this would not have happened and the three behind would have been ok. The R.S.P.C.A. always prosecuted my cases and we never failed to get a conviction.

The worst cruelty to animals case I was involved with occurred near Clitheroe Auction Mart at 7.15 one autumn morning. I was in Station Road when a three tier cattle lorry appeared from the North containing sheep. I could see the head of the sheep sticking out of the side. The lorry turned into the Auction Mart and I followed it. The sheep I had seen was in fact alright, but I opened an inspection hatch and there was a dead sheep on the floor. I told the driver to unload and when he opened the back door, sheep fell out. The maximum number the lorry should have contained was 135, but the lorry actually held 215. Four of these were dead and when the R.S.P.C.A. inspector arrived he had to shoot two more. The lorry had picked the sheep up in Aberdeen and they were destined for the slaughterhouse so no-one cared. The haulier and the owner, a butcher in Accrington, got the maximum fine. I told the court what the butcher had said to me when I rang him up: 'I haven't time to talk; I'm going to watch Blackburn Rovers.'

Shortly afterwards I was delegated to keep watch from an office in an old mill used at the time as a carpentry warehouse, as a policeman was suspected of breaking in. Suffice to say that the information we had received turned out to be true and one of our PC's was arrested and sent to prison.

There were so many comings and goings around this time. Older constables were occupying the new houses, three of them being tall men at 6 feet and four inches. One of them whose name was Moses Ainsworth was an ex-miner from Wigan who used to crouch on his heels instead of sitting. He was a great chap; very handy to have around if there was a fight. The two others were Bill and John Brewer who in spite of their surnames, were not related.

One was a ladies man and the other liked washing up at home and walking at a distance from the shop entries in the dark.

I was now often acting sergeant and I quite liked wearing the Corporal's ribbons. I had no respect for the Inspector at that time whose surname was Wright. I was dealing with an accident between two cars on the main road half way between Clitheroe and Whalley, whilst at the same time trying to keep the traffic flowing, when he drove straight past me in his car. On Saturday lunchtime he would hang around a certain street corner, knowing that the members of a gentleman's club would invite him in for a drink. But worst of all for me, was having to pedal up a steep hill to deliver his evening newspaper. The newspapers were delivered free to the police station by a local newsagent and Inspector Wright still wanted it when it was his day off.

Wilfred Pickles was a favourite on the BBC radio with his catch phrase, 'Give him the money, Barney'. One night the programme came from St Mary's Church Hall where I watched it from the back. When it was over, another policeman joined me and he said to Wilfred, "My wife would like your autograph."

"That will cost you a shilling," was his reply.

The policeman's answer to this is not repeatable, but there was no autograph!

Indecent assault

I have mentioned Jim Crabtree several times who was a detective constable and later a sergeant. He was involved in an incident in which he arrested a man for indecent assault. Normally if a male exposed himself to a female it was classed as indecent exposure; but in this case a little girl was playing on the bank of the River Ribble at Edisford when a man approached her and exposed himself. He didn't touch her but instead asked her to touch him.

She was very frightened and so did as he asked and then he disappeared. She told her mother what had happened and her mother phoned the police. Jim Crabtree found him and arrested him. Chief Inspector Fairclough at Clitheroe was the prosecuting officer and the defence solicitor was called Whipp. The defendant was found guilty and the case became known as Fairclough versus Whipp and is still known in criminal law as a test case. It was an exam question at various times in the sergeant's examinations.

New House, New baby!

Round about 1953, eight new police houses were built; four in Pimlico Road about a mile from the police station and four in Bright Street only half a mile distant. I was asked which I wanted and so I chose 29 Bright Street. It had the largest garden and was next to fields stretching up to Pendle Hill. We sold 1 Mitchell St for £800 which enabled us to furnish every room for the very first time. I filled the garden with vegetables and flowers and it was in this house in 1955, that Nan gave birth to our third child Lynne. What an amazing day that was! In the morning we had gone across the fields to pick mushrooms and crab apples. Nan had climbed many fences and stiles which obviously hadn't done her any harm and we were delighted with our little girl.

Later in 1955, I was called into the headquarters at Hutton and offered the vacant post of detective constable at Darwen. Lynne was still a baby and when I enquired about a police house, I found that it was on a steep incline with three steps up to the front door so I declined the job. I now know that this decision was the right one, as my knowledge of what the detective's life was; usually staying in the same town, and having a special pub where they congregated on many occasions wasn't for me.

It was on our return to England after a lovely holiday in Switzerland, that Paulette's husband Karl took us back to Basle. It was in the days before motorways in Switzerland

and so we had to go the 'scenic route'. Nan's niece Reina had come with us with the intention of working in England to enable her to practice her English. She had obtained a job at Queen's Park Hospital in Blackburn so that she could visit us on her day off. She became very handy on that trip to Basle as the weather worsened and a thick fog set in. We were unable to see more than ten yards in front of us and so Reina walked in front of the car for about a mile over the Pass until daylight came. A queue of cars lengthened behind us. We had quite a job at the customs in Dover trying to convince them that Reina actually had a job to come to in England. Reina and an Irish girl whom she had met at the hospital used to visit us weekly and I gathered that they had a whale of a time at Queen's Park although Reina couldn't compete with the Irish girl for her attractive looks. Reina stayed in England for a couple of years before she returned to Switzerland. Karl died around 1955 and Paulette gave me an expensive Kodak camera that she had given him as a birthday present. I never wanted another camera and I used it up until 2004. I still have it in its glossy case.

Our near miss with a drunk driver

One Saturday afternoon, I was off duty and Nan and I were pushing Lynne in her pram in Castle Street when fifty yards ahead a jeep was driven into Castle Street from a tight right hand bend from Moor Lane. It knocked a cyclist off his cycle on the nearside, swerved across the road knocking a second cyclist over; then drove over the offside pavement hitting a pedestrian. He then drove across the road back to the nearside. I had pushed Nan and the pram into a doorway. The jeep crossed the pavement in front of me and crashed into the archway of the Starkey Arms Hotel. I dragged the driver out and arrested him. A policeman on duty joined me and other pedestrians took care of the wounded. The pedestrian he had knocked over was quite badly hurt and eventually lost a leg. When I took that middle aged man out of the jeep he just grinned at me. It was the closest I ever got to assaulting a car driver and it was late evening when I finally got home. The court case lasted four and a half hours and the jeep driver was found guilty on drink drive charges.

Sport in Clitheroe

I was a keen sportsman whilst in Clitheroe. I played cricket for Chatburn, then Clitheroe; and football for Waddington, and also for Clitheroe and Burnley 'A' who played on Clitheroe's ground at Shawbridge. Playing for the latter two teams was generally when they were a man short on the day of the match as there were no substitutes in those days. The centre forward for Clitheroe, Clifford Chatburn, had won the prestigious Powderhall 100 yards sprint in Edinburgh; so if he managed to get away with the ball, nobody in the opposing team could catch him nor could we keep up with him. He became mayor of Clitheroe and I was chosen to lead his processions.

I also played football and cricket for the Lancashire Constabulary as well as cricket for the whole of the Lancashire forces when the annual match against the Yorkshire forces was held, usually on Test grounds. I was captain of the Lancashire cricket team for ten years and one year we managed to beat the Lancashire Club and Ground team which always contained at least seven Lancashire County cricketers. I once scored 96 against them at Old Trafford, but we only won once. For our divisional games, the umpire was Eddie Painter of test match fame, then a licensee in Clayton Le Moors.

Life in the Rossendale Valley

Police Sergeant, Rawtenstall 1958-1961

In 1958, we were still living at 29 Bright St. Ray was twelve years old and in his second year at Clitheroe Grammar School. Clive was eight and at St James Primary School and Lynne was only three years old. I was told that I had been promoted to Sergeant and so would be moving to Rawtenstall. Three days prior to our departure, the Deputy Magistrates Clerk said goodbye to me and we had a little chat. I knew that he lived next door to the Inspector, and perhaps I shouldn't have said what I did; but I told him that I hoped I would never again meet up with an Inspector as useless as the present one. Unfortunately, he told him what I had said and I was soon to discover his reaction to my comments. I had been standing in the front garden whilst we were waiting for the removal van, and wondering whether the next occupants would look after our little hedgehogs which came every morning for food. This had started the previous year with first one, then two and in 1958 two youngsters as well. If food hadn't been left for them, then one would scratch at the back door and Nan would find all four on the doorstep.

The appearance of the Inspector roused me from my thoughts as when I looked up, he was striding down the road towards me, swinging his cane and looking rather displeased. Stopping about ten yards away, he began his tirade. He shouted his torrent of verbal abuse at me, and every sentence contained a series of strong expletives. Eventually when he had stopped for breath, I told him to shut up and clear off. He did and I never saw him again. Five years later, when I became an Inspector myself, my duties also covered Haslingden where he had been before he had gone to Clitheroe, and I discovered that he had been disliked there!

I was delighted to go to Rossendale. The Superintendent, George Smith, was a gentle man, a director of Bury Football club and also in charge of the Constabulary team in which I had played. He and his wife were devout church goers and the off duty sergeant each Sunday evening got two hours overtime pay for picking them up and taking them to a little chapel, then back to their home after the service.

Our first family home in Rossendale was a semi-detached house in Musbury Crescent in Rawtenstall. It was on a hill and the view from the back was of Musbury Tor. There were many times when I wondered if I would ever climb it, but I never did.

Two of the constables also lived in the same street and their wives came across to our house on the very first day to see if we needed any help. Nan was taken into the hearts of all the police wives because it never mattered to her what rank I was; she treated everyone alike.

Four new police houses were built in the Balladen district and similar to the ones in Clitheroe and we moved into one, further up the same hill. Again we got on very well with our neighbours. I was one of three sergeants in Rawtenstall and the other two were almost at the age of retirement, having been there for some considerable time. I was brand new to the area, but within a month, one of them with a moustache similar to mine and had boasted it for a long time, shaved it off. His comments apparently were, "I'm not getting mistaken for Mr Wilson!" He retired soon after.

Rossendale was the smallest division in the County with only four officers: a Superintendent, a Chief Inspector and two Inspectors, one of whom was based in Bacup. The other three were based in the headquarters in Rawtenstall. Between Rawtenstall and Bacup was Waterfoot where there was a Sergeant and five Constables to cover the villages of Newchurch, Water, Lumb, Cowpe and Waterfoot. Bacup and Rawtenstall Grammar School was in Waterfoot where Ray went, but he never became attached to it. Throughout the Valley, there were numerous mills which mostly produced shoes and slippers. The factories were struggling and one mill owner told me that a full lorry load of slippers had been returned to him due to one slipper having had a minor fault.

Nan's ovary operation

Whilst we were living in Rawtenstall, Nan had the first of three operations. She collapsed with a severe haemorrhage and so I accompanied her to Barrowford Hospital near Colne in the ambulance. Doctor Lamberty was the Police Surgeon and his wife, also a doctor, quickly arrived and realised that Nan was in a serious condition. As a result of this, she had an ovary removed. Whilst in hospital, Nan was in a bed next to another policeman's wife who was suffering from a similar condition. He turned out to be the man who had taken the job in Darwen which I had previously refused.

The Astoria

The focal point in Rawtenstall was a very nice dance hall; the Astoria Ballroom on the main Burnley Road. This ran through the town centre from Manchester to Burnley, but it was narrow, only wide enough for vehicles to pass one either direction. On Saturdays the Astoria was the principal venue for the top bands in the country with the exception of The Beatles and the Rolling Stones. Friday was 'ballroom night'.

My first Friday evening on duty outside the Astoria was quite eventful. The traffic was heavy but flowing quite freely and lots of men in bow ties accompanying ladies in their evening gowns were entering the Astoria. I was standing on the pavement not far from the front door, when a limousine parked alongside me. There were two middle aged men in the front and two fur coated ladies in the back. The men got out and let the two ladies out and bearing in mind the fact that I was stood alongside them, no-one took any notice of me. By now, traffic was backed up behind the limousine whose driver locked the car and made towards the building with his companions.

"What are you going to do with the car?" I questioned quite calmly.

All four stopped dead and I got amazed looks from the ladies and angry glances from their male escorts.

"I always park here. My wife is the Lady Captain of the Golf Club," said the driver haughtily.

"You have one minute to remove your vehicle before I report you for causing unnecessary obstruction," I replied. Without another word, the passengers went inside the building whilst the driver quickly left the scene. I rather think that they had a poor evening as the following morning they had complained about my conduct. Obviously, I would have let them alight from the vehicle, then move the car; but not just park it there for as long as they thought necessary. Word must have gone round because I used to spend a lot of time near that dance hall and no-one ever tried to park there again.

The Monday afterwards, I was asked to go and see the Superintendent and he told me that they had objected to being prevented from doing something that they had always done. We then had a conversation in which I told him that I treated everyone the same and that the privileged were not dealt with any differently than normal people. That little episode was the nearest I ever got to receiving a complaint in all my thirty one years in the Police force.

Charles McKenna, a Scotsman, was well known for being drunk and disorderly and creating havoc in the dance hall and several of the staff ejected him from the building right in front of me. It took three of them and McKenna told one of them that he would kill him within twelve months. In the scuffle, I got kicked on the knee and hit on the arm with a beer glass. In court, McKenna told the magistrates that I had put a half-nelson on him and as a result he had landed in the foyer with his face on the ground. He actually landed on his back, but he spat at me so I turned him over and sat on his back. At the police station someone threw four buckets of water over me and I was hit in the chest several times. Someone then hit the back of my neck and that was my lot! When I came round, I was soaking wet and there was so much water in the cell that I was nearly swimming in it. The newspaper recorded headlines: *Violent Haslingden man fought Police Officer, Nine months jail!* We never had any trouble with him again, although he had previously been in court nine times; twice for assaulting a Police Officer.

After hours drinking

Many of the hotels and public houses allowed after hours drinking and I was usually alerted to it when doors were locked, but it was obvious from the noise inside that drinking was still going on. Often I would gain access when the door was opened to allow customers to exit and the reaction would always be the same; that of a plea of not guilty. More often than not though, the licensee, along with the guilty customers would be prosecuted and given a fine.

The after-hours drinking was going on throughout the area, not only late at night but into the early morning, so my next step was to pick one of the chief hotels. A constable and I watched through a window and saw about ten people drinking at the bar even though the door was locked. I knocked and it was quite some time before the licensee let us in, but I had been looking through the letter box and watching all the customers taking their drinks up the stairs and into the private quarters. The licensee said that they were friends of his and that he had given them the drinks free of charge. When I questioned him, he knew most of their Christian names, but did not know their addresses, so I reported him for obstructing the police in the execution of their duty and he was given a fine in court. I quickly reported three others and word soon got round that I wasn't having any messing. As a general rule, I didn't bother them within an hour of closing time and there were no cautions beyond that.

One of these pubs was The Wheatsheaf. This case was dismissed because the licensee said that she had given the men the beer because they had helped her to eject a drunk, who just happened to have been McKenna. It had been 11 o'clock before they had managed to get him out and the front door had been locked to stop him from getting back in. The licensee reported that she had asked two of the men who had helped her, to stay behind and discuss a hotpot supper which was being organised in connection with a football club and she had given them a drink. They were not regular customers and her husband; a former policeman, verified her story.

Two other hotels which were also reported for afterhours drinking were the Wellington and the Ram's Head hotels. The licensee of the Ram's Head reportedly forgot the time whilst engrossed in a television programme and subsequently allowed customers to obtain drinks after time. The newspaper reported, *'He became so interested in this* (the sport's programme), *he sat down and watched another programme. He rather forgot what was going on in the rest of the premises...'* Fog was blamed for the after-hours drinking at the Wellington Hotel. A darts team had been delayed by the fog after a match at the pub. Along with two P.C's, I had noticed that in spite of the fact that the doors were all locked, there was a great deal of noise coming from the inside of the Wellington Hotel, so when the doors were re-opened to allow a customer to get out, we went in and saw the wife of the licensee drinking with a couple of customers. In court she took the blame, telling the court that she had given them drinks whilst they were waiting for a taxi which had been delayed by the fog

Almond Crescent in 1958 was a lively place to live. There were houses on one side of the road only which looked up towards the new Balladen Primary School at the front and the hill beyond. At the rear, the view was once again of Musbury Tor, ten miles away. Our next door neighbours were P.C. Frank Fairclough and his wife Phyllis who couldn't have children, but they had a mongrel dog. It wasn't long before we had a puppy which was a replica of the dog next door. We named the pup 'Prince' and soon a black kitten appeared who we named 'Sammy'. I don't think that the cat realised it was a different species of animal to Prince as every time the dog went for walkies up the hillside, so did the cat.

Frank was one of the station duty constables at Rawtenstall and he owned one of the sloping back Chrysler cars which he used to loan out at 5/- a day. He was also a very good watch repairer. Our two families became great friends and in 1960 they went to Switzerland with us. I carried on playing football, but only with the police divisional team. I was also asked to be captain of their cricket team as I was already captain of the full county team.

A Frothy story

An unusual incident occurred in the road between Rawtenstall and Edenfield in the middle of the night. Along this road there is an incline for about a mile and I noticed that there was foam about three and a half feet high which seemed to be coming from every grate along the roadway. It was a most bizarre picture as it went upwards for about half a mile and then the foam stopped. I realised that whatever was happening was originating from somewhere on the steep hillside to the left. A telephone call came from Ramsbottom a short time later asking if we knew about what was happening in the River Irwell. It would seem that the river was also filled with foam and because of the weir, the water was frothing to such an extent that the foam was gushing over the parapets of a bridge which went over the main road. In actual fact, what had happened was that a large lorry had legitimately dumped a load of expired washing powder in a land fill site on the hillside, but unknown to the owner of this site, and after a period of rain, the powder was being washed through the rocks and had found its way underground to the roadway and thence into the River Irwell in Rawtenstall, before making its way to Ramsbottom three miles away.

Brothel keeping in Rawtenstall

There are very few Pakistani people in Rawtenstall, but Haslingden had a large population of them. I began to notice a number of their young men congregating in the centre of the town, then wandering off all in the same direction into Bacup Road and then down a little back street. I waited for them all to disappear, and then followed. A back gate was open and I could see a metal fire escape ladder from the yard to the first floor at the rear of the shop. There were men queuing on the ladder and a few in the yard. It was obvious to me that they were all visiting a brothel. I waited out of sight until all had been satisfied then when two young women in their early twenties came down, I confronted them. They admitted to me that they normally worked in Manchester but they could manage twenty clients here in the same time it took to deal with two in the city! I told them that their business in Rawtenstall was now at an end and they caught the last train back to Manchester.

After the war, Lancashire Police went on a recruiting campaign to the Shetland Islands and returned with sixteen recruits. One of them who worked in Rawtenstall was a good recruit. He and his wife went back to the Shetland Islands for Christmas, but unfortunately they forgot to turn their taps off. Their house froze up, then the pipes burst and by the time we had broken in, there was two feet of water flooding the ground floor rooms. It wasn't a very pleasant homecoming for them, but sadder still, he became the driver of a police traffic car and fell asleep at the wheel one night. He crashed the car into a wall and although he was unhurt, it was the end of his career.

Crawshawbooth

Crawshawbooth is a village just north of Rawtenstall, on the Burnley boundary. There were two village bobbies and it was a mystery to me why such a sleepy community required two policemen. Only twice did I ever have to deal with anything. The first was when the verger of the local church went missing and I found him hanging from a bell rope in the steeple.

The second took place one afternoon when a coach load of miners had stayed after time in the village pub. Most of them had had enough, but they wouldn't give me their names, so I collared their driver and told them that he was going with me to the Police Station. I have no idea what I would have done with him, but the suggestion worked as they weren't sufficiently drunk not to realise that they would be without their driver. As a result, I got every name and address. There were far too many for me to deal with so I let them get on the coach and clear off.

Bomb scares

About this time, there were numerous bomb scares which nearly always turned out to be hoax calls. However, they all necessitated the search of all types of premises including schools, dance halls and work places. I used to ask the owner of the building to instruct the people in the building to take out whatever they had brought into the building as they left. That way, I could search whatever was left inside the building. It always took some time and there was inevitably a feeling of apprehension until the area was declared safe.

Night cattle raid in Rawtenstall

'Night cattle raid in Rawtenstall' said the newspaper. *'Rustler still not found'*.

I had to round up three large cart horses which were galloping around an area close to Cloughfold. I suspected that the horses belonged to a farmer who had already ignored a warning to keep his fences intact, so impounded them in someone else's small holding. During the night, the farmer released the horses and took them back to his farm, so they weren't actually rustled. The magistrate fined him for not keeping correct records of his stock and the fences were brought up to the standard required.

A brush with stardom

Close to where we lived in Almond Crescent was a small pond and as I have always enjoyed sitting by the side of rivers watching the fish, sitting by this pond gave me the same relaxing experience. Often there was a young fellow also sitting by the pond, but he was learning his lines. We used to chat for a few minutes and I discovered that it was William Roache who was taking the part of Ken Barlow in Coronation Street. This chance meeting and subsequent acquaintance; meant that a short time later he was able to open a garden party at Waterfoot Police Station and he, at my request judged a fancy dress parade. I imaging that it could have been his first ever invitation as Coronation Street was still in its infancy then.

There were two policewomen in Rawtenstall. Edna Wigley, whose family came from Heywood was a lovely girl and had been only the second policewoman to have been appointed by Lancashire Constabulary. The other policewoman was a jovial character but not as efficient as Edna. Edna was engaged to be married to a young man called Jim Catlow who had a two-seater M.G. sports car. He was also a keen Blackburn Rovers supporter and during the football season on every other Saturday, he took me to Ewood Park. Edna was still in Rossendale when I left in 1964. She eventually married Jim and they moved to the Wirral in Cheshire. Almost fifty years later, I went to the funeral of one of the Probus members. The service was in St Michaels Church in Heywood and on entering the church, which was almost full, a sidesman told me that I probably knew someone who was sitting on the front pew so I went to the front of the church and was surprised to see Edna sitting there. She looked up, jumped up and flung her arms around me giving me a lovely kiss. Everyone in the church wondered what was happening as she was the sister-in-law of the Probus member who had died. Her husband Jim was sitting next to her. After the service we took time for a chat and she gave me her address. Sadly, Jim has since died and I haven't had the opportunity to visit her. I think that it is more than likely she has left her home.

Winston Place, the England opening batsman, lived in Rawtenstall and had a small newsagent's shop. Young Constable Finnerty was courting Winston's daughter and had received information that someone was going to break into the shop. I sat with him in the car and we waited for the thief. When he appeared, Finnerty was so excited that the car shook. We watched him break in then arrested him. It was his first criminal arrest, and the first of a long successful career as Finnerty ended his career as Chief Detective Superintendent of Lancashire Constabulary.

Cricket in Rawtenstall

During my first three years in Rawtenstall, I played cricket for Rawtenstall in the Lancashire league as did young Constable Guy. Depending on our duties, we sometimes played for the second team. The Evening News this particular day said, '*A policeman's holiday cup for junior champions, set to face 236, seconds won with Wilson not out 115 and Guy not out 91*'.

Whilst playing cricket for Clitheroe then Rawtenstall, I

was fourteen times in the Lancashire Police v Yorkshire Police matches. The first few times I played as a big hitter at No 4 or 5, then for the last six occasions as an opening batter, as I was then playing for Rawtenstall in the Lancashire league. I batted against three of the fastest West Indies professional test cricketers including Wesley Hall, Griffiths and Gilchrist, but my favourite newspaper headline was '*Wilson and Borde tame Tyson*'! Frank Tyson, as an English test player was the fastest in the world. I scored 46 before my middle stump was hit and rocketed twenty yards away, but Chandu Borde and I had scored 86 between us. Another pleasant memory is scoring 96 against Lancashire 2nd eleven at Old Trafford during the ten years I was captain of the Lancashire Constabulary. There were always first eleven batters and bowlers playing against us and one year it was Brian Statham.

Drunken driving

I arrived in the police car to attend an accident in Burnley Road, Rawtenstall where a van had crashed into a wall. The driver, who had a bandage around his head, was just being put into an ambulance. The moment he spoke, I knew that he had been drinking so I told the ambulance men that I was dealing with him and that if treatment was necessary I would take him to the hospital after he had been charged. I did exactly that about an hour later. He had a friend with him when he had crashed the van and it turned out that they had been in two different clubs. A district nurse bandaged him as he kept on saying that he had a broken neck. On the following day the Daily Express made it a full page story.

'Broken neck driver protests to his M.P. Did driver with a broken neck have to toe the white line? All the crowds at the scene wondered why he was being taken in a police car and the ambulance had gone off without him... wife says that they are complaining to the Chief Constable...'

The final court decision was, 'Broken neck driver is banned... ' He did spend ten days in hospital but if there had been a complaint, I never knew about it.

Fire Engine in a Jam

A fire engine was racing to attend a Mill fire in Bacup Road and the driver was travelling at a fast speed; too fast to turn sharp left from Burnley Road. There were lots of people about and as he tried to turn left, he ended up jammed between the shop fronts and the safety barrier at the edge of the footpath, instead of keeping on the road. I saw it happen and knew that the fire engine was unable to move. The firemen climbed out to await a second engine. Many people could have died if they had been on that busy pavement, but thankfully no harm was caused. The driver wasn't allowed to drive a fire engine again, but managed to keep his job in the fire service. It is a shame that a newspaper photographer had not been on the scene, as it would have made a wonderful photograph for the paper; the engine jammed tightly with not an inch to spare!

Police Sergeant, Waterfoot 1961-1963

We had been in Rawtenstall for three years when the Sergeant at Waterfoot police Station retired and I was asked to take his place. We moved for the third time in three years, but looking back, it was to become one of the happiest times in my life.

The police station was on the ground floor of a detached house in Bacup Road, close to the village centre. The upper floor was the Sergeant's quarters and the whole house was centrally heated. There was a very large lawn which had once been a bowling green and a flower border surrounded it. A gardener looked after the garden and the central heating. We also had a lady who cleaned the police station, and both Nan and the cleaner had their morning coffee break together upstairs. I was now 38 and I bought my first second hand car. I had previously driven Police cars, but had never before possessed a car of my own. It was a Simca saloon and carting shopping home by bus became a thing of the past. Saville's bakery was close by and the mechanic who serviced their delivery vans also serviced my car which was a great bonus. I also soon understood why some elderly constables never wanted to go beyond being a village policeman. At Christmas, a large turkey would appear, and throughout the year, sacks of potatoes. In my childhood days, I had picked mushrooms in the fields, but now we could visit a local mushroom establishment where fresh mushrooms in their thousands were available any day. There was also a tripe factory in the Valley, but I only went there once as the smell was sickening. Our lives in Waterfoot were good and we were very happy.

We were always church goers and throughout our five years in the Valley, we regularly attended Kay St Baptist Chapel in Rawtenstall. Both Ray and Clive attended Bacup and Rawtenstall Grammar School whilst Lynne went to Waterfoot Infant School which was close by. She very quickly made friends with Michael Walker who was the son of the village doctor, and John and Joyce Walker became great friends of Nan and I, a friendship which lasted until John died in the 1990's.

Although I could borrow a police car if I wanted one, I usually went about on a bicycle. I had six village constables looking after Waterfoot, Newchurch, Cowpe, Lumb and Water, but each of them had to cover the night duty in turn; which like Clitheroe meant taking telephone calls at each hour end.

Although Nan was just the village sergeant's wife, she became special to everyone she met and the superintendent arranged for her to hold a garden party. Knowing that I knew William Roache, he asked him if he would open the garden party.

The local newspaper wrote: *'Police garden party was an enormous success, despite the rain... The Police garden party scheduled to be held on the lawn of Waterfoot Police Station on Saturday afternoon had to be transferred to St James Church Waterfoot because of rain! However, after the sideshows were re-erected and the fair had been officially opened by actor Mr William Roache, Ken Barlow of Coronation Street, the afternoon proved to be an enormous success.'* This was the first of its kind to be held in the village for several years.

After hours drinking

The previous sergeant in Waterfoot had been a bit lax in his attitude to drinking after hours, but I wasn't about to change my ideas about late night drinking so two public houses, the Roebuck Inn and the Bishop Blaize, were reported about midnight. The Roebuck's defence was to explain their after-hours drinking on a birthday party. The local paper reported: *'Private Birthday plea is unavailing,'* and a total of £25 in fines was brought for the licensee. Shortly afterwards the Roebuck Inn had customers drinking after time on a Sunday afternoon. The newspaper also recorded this and said: *'Out of hours drinkers saw police sergeant's face at the window... glasses grabbed in all directions!'*

At the Bishop Blaize Hotel, we noticed that three vehicles were parked outside the hotel and the bar lounge light was still illuminated at 11:45, so we went round the back and saw, through an ornamental window, seven people round a table which had several glasses on it. The licensee assured the court that no drinks had been bought after 10:30, but the court fined the customers for drinking after hours and although the licensee was given a discharge, he was given the discharge on payment of costs.

'Volunteer's Hotel at Newchurch... nine round the bar at midnight...' was another story reported in the newspaper. A full page spread recorded; *'Raided club warned by Magistrates.'* There were twenty one men drinking in Cloughfold Working Men's club when I raided it at midnight. One hundred and sixty three summonses were issued and it took four hours in court. It is important to mention one particular licensee and his wife who had the Red Lion Hotel at Higher Cloughfold. This hotel was the rendezvous of the Newchurch Hunt where the horse riders with their hunting dogs commenced and finished their quest for foxes. I and many others had the impression that this landlord thought that he was more upmarket than the usual licensee. Several times late at night and into the early hours of the morning, I could hear customers on the premises. When I knocked on the door the lights would be extinguished and there would be no answer. I was determined that the next time would be different. I had a constable with me and found the usual lights on in the premises which I knew would soon be extinguished, but before knocking on the door I had looked through the front letter box and seen that the inner glass door was open. I could see the passage from the bar room to the stairway. I knocked and as usual, the lights were immediately extinguished in the bar, but I saw the licensee, his wife and a number of other people leave the bar and go up the stairs.

A solicitor represented them in court, but they lost the case. It was the first time that this type of summons was issued to deal with a licensee in the whole of Lancashire and possibly the country. A lot of other licensees in Rossendale clapped their hands and felt like justice had been done. The local press had a beano! '£5 fine for obstructing the police...Licensee didn't hear 1am knocks on door...' The first paragraph read: 'Licensee of the Red Lion Hotel, Ernest Trillo, was fined £5 and ordered to pay five guineas advocates fee at Rawtenstall court for obstructing the police in the execution of their duty by alleged refusal to answer continuous knocking on the door in the early hours of the morning.'

Two more licensees were reported for drinking after hours, one of them twice in a fortnight and the second time it was at 2am in the morning; several of the customers having jumped out of the back windows six feet down into the River Irwell. Drinking after time then stopped in my section.

Cases involving animals:

Dog rescue

In every policeman's life there is surely the rescue of a dog from somewhere and I was no different. The River Irwell was in flood and there were icy conditions. A woman heard a dog whining from where the river ran between two brick walls and then under the railway bridge. I was informed and I had great difficulty in climbing down and into the raging torrent. I had no idea what depth the river would be, but fortunately it was only waist high and didn't go any deeper although I had a struggle to reach the puppy which was terrified and just managing to stay on a small ledge. I carried it back to the police station and it joined me in front of a roaring fire and before long a good owner was found for it.

Bullock rescued from a well

This is a little story from the newspaper: The caption read, '*Torchlight rescue of Bullock from well.*' Police and farmers struggled in deep snow to rescue a 4 cwt bullock from a dry well at Lower Walls Farm, Lumb. The bullock was hurled eight feet to the bottom when some planks over the well collapsed. A call to the RSPCA brought the RSPCA Inspector Faulkner and Sergeant Wilson from Waterfoot to the hill farm and together with four good neighbouring farmers; ropes were fastened to the bullock which was jammed nose to tail. As the torches shone, the animal was hauled out of the well after some very hard work and apart from bruises it was unhurt. My story goes a little further. When I got back to the police station, I found that my very good wrist watch had been lost, so later in the morning I trudged back up the hillside to the well. The snow was still deep, but obviously was much flattened around the well and there was no sign of my watch. As I stood at the edge thinking sadly about the missing watch, my right foot had been moving in a left to right motion and the silver watch appeared under my moving foot. My emotions went from sadness to joy in a minute!

One morning a Diseases of Animals Inspector from the Ministry came to see me in a very agitated condition. He told me that he had been to a farm at Lumb to inspect some records and the farmer produced a shotgun and said that if he went on his land again he would shoot him. Being a D of A Inspector myself, I knew that he had the right to examine any records, so off we went. On the off chance that the farmer was serious about shooting the Inspector, I left him at the farm gate, went to the house and knocked at the door. I was rather apprehensive, and hoped that the uniform would suffice. It did because when he opened the door clutching the shotgun, he immediately put it down. The ministry man was able to do his job and I had a talk with the farmer. There had been a previous argument between them and he realised what an idiotic thing he had done as at the very least he could have lost his shotgun license. However, all I recorded was some notes in my pocket book.

This reminds me of another visit to a farmhouse on the hillside in Waterfoot. Nan and I with the children were going on a week's holiday to visit friends in Tonbridge in Kent. The day before we left, a farmer came into the police station and said that his son wouldn't let him use his car to take his milk churn the half a mile down to the main road where the milk lorry collected it. Instead, he had to use a small hand cart so I went up to the farm where the twenty two year old son was working. Apparently the son was allowed to use the car provided he put petrol in it which he did, but realised that his father didn't so the son wouldn't let him use the car. A little chat with them both over a cup of tea in the farmhouse quickly solved it. However, it's what happened after that which caused some distress. When we reached Kent the following day a rash appeared on my cheek and jaw, and after two days of severe irritation, blisters were forming so we left our friends who had children and returned home. My doctor friend told me that I had got an infection from the farm visit. Antibiotics cured it, but for two weeks I had a short beard. I never again had a drink in a farmhouse.

A case of kidnapping...

One of the picturesque routes from Waterfoot to the Burnley boundary was the four miles along the River Irwell to the moorland and the source of the river. There was a small church and a school along the way. One afternoon, I received an urgent call from the headmaster that he was being pestered by newspaper reporters. This is the story. The vicar of the village church and his wife had separated and she had returned to her own family in Glasgow, taking with her their small daughter. The vicar wanted his daughter back and so he set off in his car and went to Glasgow. He parked outside the school his daughter attended there, and then picked her up at playtime, heading straight away back to Rossendale. This disappearance was initially thought of as a kidnapping but the child's mother quickly realised that it was her husband who had taken his daughter and not a kidnapper, so her brother and a friend set off in hot pursuit. Whilst still in Scotland they pulled into a service station and saw the vicar's car. As they got out of their car, the vicar and his daughter left the café and saw them. The vicar bundled his daughter into his car and set off with the two men following as fast as they could. The vicar, whilst trying to escape, ran over his brother-in-law's foot before finally driving off. The two men were now in no position to follow the vicar and so abandoned the chase. The vicar at last arrived home and the following day enrolled his daughter in the local school.

The reporters carrying cameras and who had been pestering the headmaster were from the National newspapers and one was taking photographs of the children through the school windows and the other had actually entered the school. When I arrived at the school I got the two cameramen together and told them that if they re-entered the school premises I would report them for obstruction, but if they came to the police station later, we would tell them what I knew. They duly arrived at the police station to listen to the information I had to give them. The vicar had told me his version of what had happened and realised what a foolish thing he had done. He knew that he would be found at fault whatever court he appeared at and left the Valley most probably losing his ministry as well. I never heard what had happened in the end as no offence had actually occurred in my area.

A fisherman called in to say that he had been fishing in a lodge and his line had got caught in something solid in a deep part of the lodge and he thought it might be a safe. According to the rules, I should then have called in the Underwater Unit at Preston, but instead I asked a chap I knew in Waterfoot who did a lot of sea diving with flippers to come with me. The idea really was to get a rope fastened around it and hoist it up. It wasn't necessary as it turned out to be a fruit machine which had been stolen from an Irish Working Men's' Club in Bacup a few weeks before. We dried it out and for curiosity we played it to see how long it took for the jackpot to pay out. We would have played it for ever because the management had levelled out the cog with lead and it was never able to pay out the top award. Had the Irishmen found out, there would have been one dead body at least in the management committee. The machine was scrapped.

The railway line from Rawtenstall to Bacup ran for four miles through the stations of Cloughfold, Waterfoot and Stacksteads, before terminating at Bacup. There were porters at all the stations but the one at Bacup was a small man, older than most, who was generally ignored by passengers alighting. On Saturday nights the diesel train was packed to capacity for the last journey with teenagers and those in their early twenties, mostly dancers from the Astoria. For a laugh they would often pull the communication cord bringing the train to a stop. The Rawtenstall head station master for the valley rang me about this last train so I told him that the next Saturday I would await his call should anything occur between Rawtenstall and Waterfoot. I had a constable waiting with me and the call came that the train for Bacup full of passengers had left Rawtenstall and the communication cord had been pulled twice in the first mile before reaching Cloughfold. I told him to stop the train at Cloughfold and keep it there.

We pedalled the half a mile to Cloughfold and the train was waiting. It was jam packed with very jovial people until I said "Everybody without a ticket, get off!" I was astounded because only seven passengers actually had tickets. I told the train driver to go and off it went. Almost three hundred folk set off walking the three miles to Bacup. There was never any trouble with the train again.

Police Inspector, Rawtenstall 1963-1964

To become inspector, I had to take the Inspectors Police law exam and passed, but at some stage it was necessary to appear before a promotion board which usually consisted of three senior officers, one of whom would be the Deputy Chief Constable. Somewhere along the line I had been told that if I went before a promotion panel it would be useful to get them interested in a topic that I knew a lot about but that they knew nothing. It had worked on the PC to Sergeant Panel, as I had talked about Diseases of Animals. However on the Sergeant to Inspector panel, I had a different topic entirely. I had taken the three driving courses and obtained a First Class Advanced Driving Certificate. Whilst on one of these courses, I was driving in Edge Lane, Liverpool and was approaching a junction where the main road divided to the left and right of a church. There was a wayside pulpit right in the middle and the text on it read: 'Give a man a fish and you feed him for a day; Teach a man to fish and you feed him for life.' I had used that as my talk and it must have impressed the Board, because I was then told that I had been promoted to Inspector.

It was now necessary to move house once more, but we didn't go far. We moved into a semi-detached house which had previously been Superintendent George Smith's police house until he retired. It was still in Waterfoot and so the children were still able to attend the same schools. Unusually, I stayed in the same division. Inspector Helsby was sent to Burnley and I took his place in Rawtenstall. On my first day as Inspector I found myself in charge of the whole division as the other three officers were away. I now had to find my feet as Prosecutor in court, but I was ably assisted by the Magistrates Clerk.

Nan was obviously delighted at me going up a step in the promotional ladder, but as usual she didn't alter, continuing in her pleasant way and she still looked after the tea and biscuits at cricket matches as I continued playing. It meant that I had to be fitted for a dress suit as now we were expected to attend different functions with the other officers. Annually, the police organised an amateur boxing night in the Astoria ballroom. It was always packed out and all the officers in the Division had to attend in evening dress. This was the first time I had ever worn a dress suit and this one lasted me until I retired in 1977. This was not bad for one dress suit, but Nan made up for it by having a new dress on every occasion! One of my other duties was to visit all the pharmacists twice a year to inspect their drug registers and assess the security of the drugs. I had my own office and we always had an 'open door' which it hadn't been previously. One of the nice things about the officer rank was being able to discard the black boots and be able to wear shoes. The ebony stick was also a pleasant asset and car allowance was obviously a bonus. There were no more night duties although I occasionally stayed out until midnight.

Valley closed off by floods

One Saturday morning, storm clouds appeared in Rossendale; the sky went black and it began to hailstone very heavily and every drain on the roadsides in Rawtenstall, Waterfoot and Haslingden became blocked with the hailstones. It then rained heavily, storm force for several hours. The main roads in a northerly direction – Waterfoot to Burnley, Rawtenstall to Burnley and Haslingden to Accrington were completely blocked and traffic came to a stop on all three routes. No vehicles could get in or out of the valley at the northern end. With the drains blocked, water built up and the flooding of houses became serious. If that alone wasn't enough, a reservoir above Haslingden then burst and the whole reservoir drained as a torrent of water came down from the hillside across the main road at Baxenden with such force that some houses were completely demolished and a car on the road was swept one hundred and fifty yards then deposited onto the railway embankment on the Bury to Accrington line. An old lady was killed and another old lady needed to be rescued from her flooded house.

After several hours the rain stopped, the hailstones melted and traffic was resumed. I returned back to DHQ tired, wet through and I saw the Chief Inspector who was immaculate and perfectly dry and I realised that he had never left his office. Haslingden is possibly the highest town in Lancashire and it is often a breezy place, so when it snows it gets more than its fair share. It also gets a lot of rain and in another incident there, a hole appeared in the main road that was big enough to have held two double decker buses.

For the next year we had a lovely time with the numerous friends we had made, and to me as a young Inspector it was a learning period. Two of Nan's sisters and a niece with her fiancé came on holiday from Switzerland and suddenly it was time to move again. Superintendent Parrott was promoted to Chief Superintendent of Bolton Division and as there was a vacancy for an Inspector in charge at Horwich he asked if I would go with him. The Chief Inspector at Rawtenstall, Lou Smith was also being promoted to Superintendent in charge at Rawtenstall Division and he said, "Don't take Jack Wilson away, I need him here." It put me in a quandary but a discussion with Nan made my mind up to accept the move to Horwich. However, I wasn't given time to give them my decision because a message came from Sir Archibald Horderne the Chief Constable, saying that I was to go to Heywood which was the toughest town of its size in Lancashire, and I had to sort it out. Little did I know at that time that we would like the people of Heywood so much, and that we would stay at our home in Jesmond Dene for as long as God would allow.

Heywood 1964 – 1977

1964 – Our new home…

Nan and I went over to Heywood to see 'Jesmond Dene';
the house we would call home for the foreseeable future.
Little did we know at the time just how long this house
would be our family home. We had driven over the moors
from Edenfield, seen the sign to Heywood from opposite
Knowl Hill and travelled through Ashworth Valley to
Queen's Park Road. The sun was shining and St Luke's
Church was ahead of us as we crossed the lovely bridge
with the park on our left and it looked delightful. Walking
up the road ahead was a very smart young policeman. I
stopped and asked him where his Inspector lived and he
asked me if I was their new Inspector. This Constable,
P.C. Vic Swinney became a very efficient constable and
later a dog handler Sgt, and we were involved together in
numerous incidents.

We found our destination on the Middleton side of the
town, a semi-detached house with the Grammar School
playing fields alongside and a view to the front of Knowl
Hill, fields and the town below with St Luke's Church
about a mile in the distance. It was very impressive and we
knew we were going to enjoy living there. Our neighbours
were Herbert and Susan Bold and their son David. Herbert
was the head sales rep at Transparent Paper Mills and
Susan, a music teacher, was the conductor of the Heywood
Townswomen's Guild choir. They were great friends until
it came to 'death do us part'.

My predecessor, Boydell, had lived in the Inspector's
quarters in Heywood Police Station but had been able to
purchase 'Jesmond Dene' for the police and he
subsequently moved in. It is incomprehensible why he
didn't buy it for himself, as in 1971 I was able to buy it
from the Police for £4,400. A five barred gate was the
entrance to what looked like 'no man's land', bounded by

four very large Hawthorne trees. I removed the gate and layered the bushes and with the addition of beech and laurel it became my front fence. It took about two years and with the assistance of the Highways Department, who deposited some unwanted tarmacadam and the loan of a road roller, parking space for several cars became available and the transformation was complete.

A few years later, the leasehold ground rent of £4 annually, became freehold for the sum of £40, a real bargain. In the early 1970's the new Grammar School was built in Newhouse Road and all the open fields, previously a golf course had become a housing estate for thousands of people. This meant a busy road in front of my fence. I asked to see the plans and found that we were the first two houses in a cul-de-sac, which at a future date would extend into the playing fields. It also meant that the Bold's and I would have to pay hundreds of pounds to pay half the cost of the road. I was already aware that 'no man's land' was mine as the five barred gate had prevented access to the land for more than the number of years necessary to claim it. I also reminded them that the bridle path outside the fence running alongside the school playing fields would have to remain. Common sense prevailed and Links Road continued outside my boundary and the 'S' bend into the estate was created.

In 1973, Nan thought it would be nice if we replaced the French door from the dining room into the garden with a 50% extension. A cotton mill owned by a Rotarian friend was being demolished and so the pitch pine and maple wood from the mill was given to me. One of the sergeants who had been a bricklayer, and a constable who had previously been a plasterer, combined with a local authority joiner built my new extension in their spare time. Not only was it quickly established but all my fire places were taken out and boarded up at the same time.

I knew that I was replacing Inspector John Boydell, but hadn't realised that I had seen him before. Previously, when the Clitheroe police cars needed petrol, we used to go ten miles to Church near Accrington, and Boydell, who was a sergeant at the time, always seemed to be hanging about in the office. On November 20th 1964, we came to Heywood and the following day I commenced duty in what I still refer to as 'my police station'. It was built in 1935 in Hind Hill Street opposite the Grammar School and next to the General Post Office... the ideal spot close to the town centre. The Inspector's house was at one end (then the CID) and two constables' homes were at the other end. There was a majestic staircase leading up to the upper floor where three magistrate's courts and a coroner's court could be found. This floor was later used in the Waterloo Road television programme.

I had a staff of three sergeants, eighteen constables, a CID sergeant and four detective constables, a policewoman and two dog handlers with their Alsatians 'Satan' and 'Shane'. If there ever was a dog aptly named it was Satan. Irene Forbes was the office typist; there was an odd job man who was also the mortuary attendant and two lady cleaners. Eight Specials were also available when required. In the rear yard was a weights and measures Inspector's office, three garages and a petrol pump which was also available to ambulances and a small enclosure with a kennel for stray dogs.

My first duty was to visit Chief Superintendent Halhead who welcomed me into his division. He told me that Colonel St Johnston, the Chief Constable of Lancashire had chosen me to be the sub division Inspector of the toughest town of its size in Lancashire and I was to deal with it in my own way. Providing nothing went wrong, I would be left alone. He mentioned the two Manchester City overspill neighbourhoods of Langley, just over the Heywood/ Middleton border and Darnhill; and the constant battles and trouble between the two of them. There was an unhappy feeling between the C.I.D. and beat patrols.

Chief Superintendent Halhead also told me briefly about Martha Hardy, who had been missing for twelve months; a case which was eventually to haunt me for many years. Then finally he informed me about lost property which was missing from the police station. He did not mention the carnage caused by hooligans at Christmas and New Year in the town centre. I returned to Heywood knowing that only the Chief Superintendent and probably his deputy would know why I was replacing Boydell, and also that it was going to take some time to solve one or two problems, but immediate action was needed for the rest. I was also very pleased to have been especially picked for the job. Much later on in my life, in 2013, I spoke to an old colleague of mine, a retired dog handler, about Boydell and asked him for his opinion of him. These were his words, *"I joined Heywood in 1964 and it was six months before he had a proper talk with me. His office door was always closed and he never got involved. He was a snob!"* A few more disrespectful comments were also added.

I saw all four sergeants that first day, all in the later years of their police career. On the second morning I was taken around the boundary between Rossendale, Rochdale, Middleton and Bury by Sgt Horace Percival who had for many years been the County Drill Sergeant. The area was particularly beautiful in Ashworth Valley which had a village policeman who got around using a scooter.

As we were crossing the Pilsworth area and passing some farm land, I noticed that quite a number of rabbits were running about, all colours and obviously not wild rabbits. I asked Percival why they were in the field and he told me that the farmer bred rabbits for eating. I asked him to drive up to the farm and when we got there, I noticed that the buildings were in a very derelict condition. There were lots of rabbit pens, but no water or food. All the penned animals were either dead or dying and so I asked

121

the sergeant to get the R.S.P.C.A. Inspector up there immediately, then get the owner and report him for causing unnecessary suffering to the number of animals he could count. I said that I would give evidence. The owner was given the highest fine and ordered never again to have animals.

Whilst we were out and about that day, the sergeant said to me, "whatever you do Sir, keep away from Mrs Burton; a lady who often comes into the station. She will ask to see you and will insist that her mother has been murdered, but the case is only a missing from home". I told him that anyone who came into the police station and asked to see me would be seen, not ignored. This was a shock to him and the case eventually became one of Heywood's most notorious.

Our tour ended by travelling past the seven depots of the 35 maintenance unit of the R.A.F. which had employed three thousand civilians in the war and had a personnel of thirty three police. On the Wednesday, I received a lovely welcome from the chairman of the magistrates, the clerk of the court, a barrister, a solicitor and a journalist from the press. In the afternoon, I went to the town hall and was greeted by the Mayor and Mayoress; George and Irmgard Dobson, and all the chief officials of the town council. I had a glass of wine with them and I thought, 'this is great, it could be a very pleasant existence.'

I was in the enquiry office, examining the Lost and Found property books, when a middle aged lady came in and she looked very surprised when she saw me. It turned out to be Mrs Burton, the daughter of Martha Hardy and she was even more surprised when I took her into my office and gave her a cup of tea. I listened to her account of the story and it was obvious that there was no love lost between her and her mother as she had been left out of her mother's will. She claimed that her mother had been murdered and that her mother's sister, Miss Brassington had also been murdered a few months after her mother. Two names were given to me and she left the Police

Station knowing that if anything came to light, we would contact her. I will recount this story in more detail later.

Within a few days of my arrival, a Chief Inspector from the R.A.F. Police called with an invitation from the Group Captain to make me an honorary member of the R.A.F Officers' mess, which I accepted. I was to alter my abstinence of potent drinks. It was in December when Nan and I received an invitation to a banquet in the Officers' Mess at 35 M.V. It is a good thing that men can use the same dress suits as it was yet another new gown for Nan. We were picked up by the Mayor and Mayoress accompanied by Mr and Mrs Ronald Parker, the town clerk and we arrived in style at the Officers' quarters. A large marquee was the venue and we were greeted by Group Captain Southgate, two squadron leaders and twenty two other officers and their wives. Another guest was the Bishop of Middleton and his wife. He was a little man who looked quite regal in his black frock coat and gaiters.

The first drink of the evening was ladled out in liberal amounts from a very large crystal bowl. It was punch, very nice indeed and on being asked if we would like a refill, the Bishop and I had a second glass. Apparently, up until that evening, the Bishop had been tee-total. The gorgeous meal along with a plentiful supply of wine; the glasses of the unwary being topped up, lasted for three hours. It got warmer and warmer in the marquee and I remarked that I needed to cool down. The Bishop also wanted some air, and Nan urged us not to go out into the cold air, but we did. The freezing air hit us like a ton of bricks and we wobbled. He'd had as much to drink as I, but was only half my size, so before he collapsed, he grabbed hold of me and we re-entered the tent with our arms clasped around each other. We got a rousing reception from the R.A.F. but we must have looked a bonny sight. Back at home that night, Nan had a few quiet words to say, and as she had kept strictly to her code of drinking a maximum of one glass of wine whatever the occasion, I have adhered to that same code ever since.

All the senior officers of the R.A.F lived in the R.A.F owned houses in Jackman Avenue, across the playing fields from us. A Squadron Leader invited us to his Christmas party, which we attended. The Maintenance Unit was comprised of seven different units in the Heywood area, each controlled by several R.A.F officers, which meant a constant stream of personnel either coming or leaving. This was always an excuse for a party in the Officers' Mess at the H.Q. in Pilsworth. We were always invited and always went, but Nan had to manage with her dresses from earlier Police balls. The units were supervised by R.A.F. police. They had thirty three, several more than I had to cover the town of Heywood.

Several issues necessitated my immediate attention:

1. Although technically under the supervision of the Detective Inspector at Bury, the C.I.D Sergeant and his four detective constables were working in my police station and I insisted that every morning I was informed of the latest crime situation and what was happening. I also insisted that if the Sergeant and his detectives received information from the beat bobbies which resulted in an arrest, then the bobbies were to be given the credit and not the C.I.D.

2. The traffic branch had to come in for petrol and to join in the general work of getting the town back to normal, and help with the hooligans. This was quickly achieved.

3. The missing lost property was several found pedal cycles. They may have been given away to a deserving cause, but should have been dealt with legitimately.

4. The beat bobbies were mostly young recruits, but one of the senior constables considered himself to be a 'ladies' man' and for quite a while had an affair with the wife of a council member. As he was eligible for retirement, I let him know that I was not impressed and within a few months, he had retired and left Heywood. He and his family occupied one of the two houses attached to the

police station. The other police house was also unoccupied so they became part of the police station.

5. The Seven Stars public house was the only one of its kind in East Lancashire and well into Yorkshire, having a disco dance hall. It was notorious for the rowdy behaviour of its clientele at closing times on Friday and Saturday nights. It was next to St James Church and a complex of two storey apartment buildings. The mayor and his family occupied one of the houses. On the first Friday night, the sergeant, three constables and I dealt reasonably well with the locals, but we had one in each of the five cells for disorderly conduct, something that had not happened for several years. But Saturday night was different. My small task force was augmented by a dog handler from Bury. Three coaches were parked outside, one each from Huddersfield, Bradford and Wakefield; presumably calling en-route from the coast back to Yorkshire. By the noise inside the pub, there was little doubt that there was going to be a battle, not just between the red rose and the white rose, but also white versus white.

The handler who was looking after a second police dog brought his own dog out of one of the two compartments in his van. Our own transit was soon on its way to the police station, filled with drunk and disorderly conduct prisoners. The handler also had a prisoner and having no transit van decided his client would travel by dog van. He opened the van door and bundled him into the empty half, or so he thought, pushing him into the one with the other dog in it. The animal must have thought he was getting a special treat and immediately bit him. There was a loud shout of pain and he stumbled out, trousers torn and blood dripping down his leg. We patched him up with the first aid kit, then after telling the handler not to worry, I took the patient off to Bury General Hospital. The nurse, on being told that he had been bitten by a police dog said, "serve him right, I will get a big needle!" Shortly afterwards there was another shout of pain. The following morning, when the prisoner was charged with being drunk and disorderly, he had no idea how he had been bitten and pleaded guilty.

It must have permeated through the coach firms that Heywood wasn't the best place to stop as within a few more weeks, they stopped calling. The stupid behaviour of the locals took rather longer to stop altogether.

In all the other places I had served, New Year's Eve had always been a joyous occasion, but that had apparently not been the case in Heywood for several years. People used to congregate and sing carols around the large Norwegian spruce tree in the town centre, until hooligans spoiled the fun. Hundreds of people were leaving the pubs as New Year approached; and as the town clock struck and St Luke's bells chimed, I saw the top half of the Christmas tree bending downwards. Someone had previously tied a strong rope to the top and a gang were pulling it. As traffic went along York St, they released the rope and hundreds of light bulbs cascaded outwards, many of them shattering against a passing ambulance. A large shop window was also shattered by a brick.

There were many arrests, and several suffered dog bites. They complained about being bitten, but I told them that if they had not been in the centre of the fracas, they would not have been bitten, and I was not interested in their complaints. Other than an odd drunk, there was no further trouble as the years passed by. Nan and I received invitations to attend all three Conservative Club Christmas parties and they were all very friendly with brass bands or choirs as their entertainment.

Our neighbours were the Bold family and as we began to know the many of the residents of Heywood, we quickly had a large circle of friends, particularly Nan. Ray transferred his workplace from 'Smith and Nephew' to 'James Kenyon's' in Bury and Clive and Lynne were pupils at Heywood Grammar School which moved from Hind Hill Street to a new building in Newhouse Road, only two hundred yards away from our house.

'Hill Top' was an old detached house in a small copse of trees sixty yards away. A small footpath led from my entrance along the front of the garden alongside the rough abandoned allotments with a small pond, until half a mile distant when it passed under the railway line at Pothole, and thence into the town streets. This was a short cut for me to the police station but there was not sufficient space for a car.

The occupant of 'Hill Top' was Mrs Edwards, the widow of Group Captain Edwards who had been C.O. of 35.M.U. They had a daughter who had been a debutante and there was a granddaughter called Victoria. Mrs Edwards was fond of Nan and they often chatted together. She was a millionaire, but treated Nan as an equal in society. She appreciated me as a Police Inspector and I did assist her in keeping her boundary fence in good order. Mrs Edwards invited us to some of her special event dinner parties either at the 'Crimble' or the 'Normandy' hotels and she tipped very lavishly. On one visit to the Crimble she had twenty guests. When I asked the waiter for a well done steak, he told me that they didn't serve over-done meat. It would have been impolite to tell him what to do with his meat, so I kept my mouth shut.

Mrs Edwards was obviously the 'Belle of the ball' during her first marriage as the wife of a high ranking R.A.F. officer. Her second marriage was to a retired Police Constable who was a rich man due to buying cinemas and converting them into Bingo halls. They moved into a large modern house in Bamford with a large garden, but her husband died within a few years. She was a regular attender of evensong at St Luke's Church and when she was unable to drive her car anymore, I used to take her to and from church every Sunday.

It was after Nan had died and I was seventy two when she invited me out to dinner and I was asked to be at her home for 7pm. Lynne dropped me off and in my best suit and clutching a bunch of flowers I knocked at the door. I had told Lynne to make some excuse and to come and pick me up at 10 o'clock. I nearly died when the door opened and she was dressed in a long black ball gown which was extremely low cut, and round her neck hung a string of pearls, resting on bare flesh.

I was escorted into a large lounge and there on a small table were a decanter, not a bottle of wine, and two glasses which obviously indicated that only two people were dining; her and me. I think it was during the hour we spent drinking and conversing that she told me that she had left her first husband for a few months and in that time she had had a fling with someone else. It was just as well that by this time in my life I had become immune to the intoxicating effects of drinking wine.

We then moved into the dining room and she served a gorgeous meal. I sat at the lower end of a fifteen foot long table and she was at the top. Thank goodness Lynne rang the bell at 10 o'clock as I reckon I was in line for husband number three! I would have become a rich man. I did find out that she was being diddled to some tune by her two landscape gardeners, so I got her to sack them and found her someone I knew. I saw him later and he said it was the best job he had had. Every time he was due, there were two bottles of beer waiting for him in the shed. Sadly she died about seven years ago. She was a very nice lady, always well dressed and she was a good parishioner as she gave money to necessary projects. Her brothers owned part of the Tyneside shipyards and several woollen mills in Yorkshire. I used to take flowers from my garden to her grave in Heywood Cemetery as her own daughter lives near Inverness in Scotland.

During my first few months in Heywood there were so many things happening both to Nan and I. I wandered round with the sergeants and constables and chatted to all different types of folk. Business people stopped ringing Bury Police and rang me instead. I visited all the mills and business premises and in 1965 I was invited by a member of the Rotary Club who was a town councillor, to become a member. Immediately I made another thirty three

128

friends. The wives of the Rotarians also invited Nan into their Inner Wheel Club and so she also increased her circle of friends. In time she became the President of the Inner Wheel and held that position for two years.

Besides looking after our three children, Nan became involved with Cancer Research, the Blind Welfare Centre and the Lifeboat Society. She started a whist drive group with twenty ladies who had a whist drive in their different homes every fortnight and the half-crown (worth 12 ½ p today) entrance fee was given to charity. She was the interpreter for the Official Twinning with the German town of Peina (unpaid) and also the Interpreter for the Townswomen's Guild Choir in five languages as well as organising the policemen's wives to meet once a month at the Police Station. I wish she could have helped me in the garden, but she thought it was much nicer to cut the flowers and hand them on to all the deserving causes.

Returning to policing, I had a little innovation that worked wonders. If children mis-behaved, and were brought into the police station, they were sat out of the sight of the public in the front office which was always manned 24 hours a day and the parents had to come and collect them. We never had a child coming twice.

Heywood was one of the first towns in the County to encounter glue sniffers. A group of parents came to see if I could do anything to stop their children sniffing glue as they were climbing on the roof of the library building believing they could fly. They were in their early teens. This was a new one for me and so I thought carefully for a few minutes, then asked the parents if they would agree to me charging their children with 'behaviour likely to cause a breach of the peace'. It would mean them appearing before the magistrates at the Juvenile Court but the parents agreed. They duly appeared and were bound over to keep the peace for twelve months and it worked. I sent a letter to the Home Office asking what damage glue sniffing could cause and was given the information that it could cause brain damage. All the shopkeepers in Heywood were asked if they would refuse to sell glue to children and they all complied with our request. Glue sniffing subsequently ceased in Heywood.

In the ten years I was in Heywood, I only had two complaints. One was about the dog handler and the other concerned a Traffic Sergeant. He liked a drink and one day he was sitting in his car, having imbibed somewhat, when two of his traffic colleagues saw him and wanted to take him home to sober up, but he was adamant that he could drive so they took him to the police station. He was demoted to Constable and was sent to work for me. Patrolling Darnhill on a bike was ideal for him as he really was a good bobby. It was a detached beat and he was very capable of dealing with the locals. He was cycling slowly along and as he passed three boys in their middle teens who were sitting on a wall with their legs dangling, they said something which he didn't like and so caused him to stop. He laid his bike on the path and paced slowly towards them without saying a word. Then he hit the nearest one, sufficiently hard enough to create a domino effect and they all fell off the wall. Apart from their egos, none of them was hurt. I wasn't aware of this until the following morning when the enquiry office constable told me that a Member of Parliament wanted to see me. I told him to bring him in and rustle up two cups of coffee. He was a Member of Parliament for Sheffield and was in Heywood visiting a brother. One of the lads was his nephew and he was quite irate when he told me his version of the story, but the coffee soon calmed him down. I explained to him that although there were a number of decent families living on the estate and there was little doubt that his was one, if they wanted to live in peace then that constable needed to work the Darnhill beat. Instead of an official complaint, I asked him to let me deal with it and he agreed. I did have a few words with George, "don't hit them so hard next time!"

A distressing event in Darnhill was never recorded. A young lady of about 20 came to see me, explaining that her mother had died some years previously and that she lived with her father. I listened to her sad story of incest. I told her he would be arrested and probably be in prison for a long time and went immediately to see him with the knowledge that she would not give evidence against him. He listened to what I had to say, accepted his guilt, packed his bags and left the house to his daughter. As far as I know, she never saw him again. There was never any record made or recorded of that dreadful episode, and up until now I have never mentioned it.

Promotion

Promotion was always very pleasant and after four years as Inspector I felt ready for the next step upwards, but a disastrous thing happened regarding my prospects. In all the towns in Lancashire where an Inspector was the top policeman he would be regarded as the local Chief Constable, always on duty sometimes for twelve to fourteen hours daily depending how lively the district was. I didn't mind how many hours above the normal eight hours I worked, but apparently many Inspectors were grumbling. Mr Palfrey, the Chief Constable who knew me very well, decided to stop the grumblers by moving every town Inspector to the divisional offices, and all would work the three shifts round the clock. Normally I would cover Heywood for the whole of the day, completing shifts each morning, afternoon and evening. Now I was working an eight hour shift and based in Bury. The other sixteen hours each day I would be off duty. If anything happened in Heywood, I would of course attend to it, but the whole day was not covered as well as it had been. The Magistrates in Heywood, (whose chairman was a friend of Mr Palfrey), the Magistrate's Clerk, Mayor and Councillors, Coroner and many, many others were extremely disgruntled and the Chief Constable, Mr Palfrey received more complaints about me leaving to work in Bury than he did from all the other towns in Lancashire. I knew that it was an unworkable plan and my comment: "This is never going to work. It's crazy!" which I made to one of the magistrates, was eventually passed on to Mr Palfrey and he believed that I had been trying to stir up trouble, which wasn't true of course.

When I worked in Bury and on night duty, I used to spend the first two hours in Heywood, then after midnight quite often I would walk the four miles or so to Bury. On one such evening when it was approaching Christmas, numerous homes had Christmas trees in their windows. I had just crossed the river at Heap Bridge and as I was passing a row of houses, a tree that was lit with candles was still burning and had set fire to the curtains. It blazed up as I dashed to the front door and hammered on it. Within seconds the door was opened and so together with the owner we were able to quench the fire with water. Both curtains were alight and I probably saved their lives that night.

A second memorable incident occurred during nights at Bury. At 2am one morning I was walking with a constable when we saw smoke billowing out from the market hall. It was on fire. I called the Fire Brigade, but there was no possible chance of putting out the fire. Several fire engines were quickly on the scene, but the building was destroyed. I realised that I needed the Transit van to use as a base, as within half an hour several insurance assessors and stall holders were congregating and getting in the way. Within two hours I counted ten assessors and hundreds of people were watching as the stall holders lost their property. Bury of course lost its old market and the town centre was then modernised to its present position as possibly the best market in the country. There were of course two little perks to working in Bury on nights. A Chinese chippy supplied the suppers and Benson's toffee factory supplied very cheap toffees once a week!

Within a few weeks Mr Palfrey had to send all the Inspectors back because as I had predicted, it just didn't work, and of course he blamed me. He didn't say anything to me until four and a half years later and I was one of twenty Inspectors from different forces on a college course at Hutton. Mr Palfrey was the guest of honour and I was sat only two seats away from him, so just after the piper piped in the haggis, he leaned forward and said to me, "Wilson, have you learned your lesson?" In reply, I told him that I knew he had blamed me. He then told me, in front of the other Inspectors, that I would be promoted to Chief Inspector. Gasps could be heard from some of the Inspectors. A few weeks later he visited Bury Division on his last day of duty before retiring, and all the officers of the division were in Chief Superintendent Tomlinson's office. As he picked up the phone, he turned to me and said, "Your wife is called Nan isn't she?" As she answered the phone, he told her that he had just made me Chief Inspector. I have no idea what she said in reply; probably 'thank you.'

Chief Inspector Wilson...

Satan and Shane – our four legged friends

Borrowing a dog from Bury wasn't working so two of my constables, Vic Swinney and Bob Cameron were dispatched to the training school and came back; Cameron with a brown Alsatian named Shane, and Swinney with a jet black Alsatian named Satan. They were both excellent at tracking but what a difference in temperament; Shane peaceful and cuddly and Satan, a demon.

The handlers were on different shifts. In the Lancashire Constabulary burglar alarms were fitted in the enquiry offices. All was silent at the premises but when intruders broke into the buildings the alarm would be raised at the police stations and this usually ended in an arrest. It was also the advent of mobile phones which each man carried. Together with the new Panda cars this made mobility and communication between men amazing.

The first apprehension for Shane was when the burglar

alarm at a rope works went off and Cameron and I went in a Panda car to Healey's Mill. The office door had been forced and in went Shane. Very quickly there was a loud cry from a youth who had his back to a wall and Shane was on his back legs with his front legs resting on the thief's chest. He was after the safe but all he had stolen were four office keys. Mr Healey, a local magistrate arrived very quickly. He was notoriously very careful with money, but I remember this case, not for the fact that it had been Shane's first arrest, but when I asked Mr Healey for one of the keys for evidence, it took him ten minutes to untie the knots, hand one to me and then re-tie the string again. This was a building with thousands of miles of string within a few feet and scissors in sight.

Police dogs have always been a very useful tool when apprehending burglars and Satan was no exception. Constable Swinney was once in pursuit of a burglar with Satan at his side. They followed his track in Heap Bridge, but the trail went cold by the River Roch just before the river ran under the main road. At this point, the water from about two miles around emptied into the River Roch and a large amount of debris often collected there. Tyres along with other rubbish created an island in the middle of the river. Satan went into the water in his urgency to find his prey, but came back out unsuccessful. The river bank was searched downstream towards Radcliffe without any trace of the burglar being found. Constable Swinney decided to give Satan a second chance to search where they thought the burglar had disappeared by the debris in the river. To his amazement, he eventually sniffed out the unlucky burglar who by this time must have been very uncomfortable. He had been totally immersed under the water, with the exception of his head, which was inside one of the tyres and covered by twigs.

A theft from the new Civic Hall being erected lead to another quick detection, this time with lead thieves. It was so nice to be in contact with everybody by phone, just to send a handler and dog inside. Late one night, an intruder set off the alarm at the Post Office at the junction of Green Lane and Rochdale Road East. The burglar was armed with a shotgun. The postmaster, who was sleeping upstairs, came downstairs and the shotgun was fired but the pellets showered the ceiling. The intruder ran off. Swinney and Satan were quickly at the scene and Satan set off up Green Lane in pursuit. Thankfully he wasn't able to trace the burglar, nor could Vic. This was the first of the Black Panther's post office burglaries. The second was when he murdered the postmaster at Baxenden near Accrington, this being the first of several terrible murders.

The Romany type of gypsy who travelled around the country lanes with a dog and several horses were never any trouble, but the Irish travellers with new motor vehicles and caravans who chose to park wherever they wanted to, were pests. On their arrival, I used to send round a couple of Bobbies; preferably a dog handler; and they had instructions to book them for whatever they could – usually no road tax or insurance. The offenders were told that a warrant of arrest would be available the next day. This always worked as the following day the sites would be clear of travellers, but not of their rubbish. This was always left for the Local Authority to clear up. These travellers rarely returned.

Occasionally, when there was no Bury Inspector available, I used to supervise Bury F.C's Second Division football matches at Gigg Lane. Those were the days in the original second division when they played Manchester City, Bolton, Liverpool and Sheffield Wednesday etc. Just before half time on one of these occasions, the tannoy at the ground announced, 'would Inspector Wilson please return immediately to Heywood!'

I left immediately in a traffic car and en-route I radioed Preston H.Q. and asked the Inspector what the fuss was all about. He informed me that a naked woman had run out of a house on the 'Back 'O the Moss' estate, and a man with a rifle was threatening to shoot anyone close by.

When we arrived, there were a considerable number of residents gathered, together with a constable and Swinney with Satan. They were all about fifty yards away from a small semi -detached Council house. A bare chested man was standing against the open upstairs bedroom window pointing a rifle upwards. I ascertained that he was the husband of the naked lady whom he had chased, but she was nowhere in sight. I tried to get him to put the gun down before I could join him, but he refused.

It was clear that we had to get the gun off this man, so I told the constable to keep him talking at the window whilst Swinney and I accessed the house through the rear. We knew that if we could get up the stairs whilst he was distracted by the constable at the front, there was a good chance that we could get to him before he turned round. It was a risk that we had to take. The rear door was unlocked and so we crept up the stairs very quietly. I could still hear the gunman talking and so we crashed the bedroom door open and very quickly hurtled into his back. The gun flew out of his grasp and arms and legs seemed to be everywhere, trapping the gunman beneath us.

Satan then did what he had been trained to do and grabbed the nearest morsel, which just happened to be Swinney's rear end! Swinney cried out and as Satan recognised his handler's voice, he relaxed his grip only leaving a minor wound on Swinney's rear.

The gun turned out to be a very powerful air rifle and Swinney dealt with the several offences which had been committed. The husband and wife eventually patched things up and so it was mission accomplished!

Bank Robbery

In broad daylight, three men robbed one of the town centre's banks, jumped into a waiting car in the side street next to the bank and drove off. The car they were in was equipped with a radio which was tuned to the Lancashire Constabulary's traffic frequency. One of my staff, Alan

Thompson, at my recommendation had been promoted to Sergeant and he took the local call from the bank. He was able to obtain the make and colour of the get-away vehicle, but no-one had seen the registration number. Immediately, he contacted Lancashire H.Q. with a request to block all the main roads out of the town. Our own two Panda cars plus two traffic cars blocked the four main roads within minutes. It may cross your minds that not much could be done by one policeman against three bank robbers, who were in all probability dangerous, but in this situation, no thought is given to the danger, only the apprehension of the criminal.

Now, the robbers were listening in to the radio, and believing they were within the blocked off area, they abandoned their car just outside the Heywood boundary, beyond the Three Arrows on the road to Whitefield. A comprehensive description of the three robbers had been obtained and the abandoned car was found. One man was apprehended crossing the fields towards Middleton, and the second was detained on Whitefield Railway Station. It was now time for Constable Swinney and Satan to do their work. They set off at a gallop following a scent which was probably the scent of one of the two men already in custody as two hours later, they returned, covered in mud with Satan looking absolutely worn out! There were a number of us still near the abandoned car and close to several police cars, when Satan's ears suddenly pricked up. He dived into a ditch about thirty yards away and sank his teeth into the nearest part of the third robber's anatomy! He had been hiding so close to us and listening to what was going on. This just proved to me what a great Section I was commanding, even when I wasn't personally involved. What a terrific ending.

A case of mistaken identity!

I received a message that the licensee of the Black Bull Inn on Rochdale Road East had been shot! As I entered the

137

Inn, I was followed by two ambulance men. The sight before me was quite bizarre. Lying in front of the bar was a man with a gunshot wound in his groin. It was quite obvious that he was bleeding to death, but all around him customers were still sitting drinking their pints of beer apparently unaffected by the incident which had just unfolded before their eyes. The ambulance men quickly took him away, but unfortunately he died before reaching Rochdale Infirmary.

I was informed that the gunman had disappeared towards Rochdale and he was arrested just inside their boundary. He was a Polish man who been in the pub the previous day causing trouble and the licensee had told him not to come back again. Obviously feeling aggrieved, he had returned that day to settle the score and shoot the man who had confronted him. However, the man he had shot was not the licensee, but the licensee's brother who was of similar build and appearance. It was obvious from the moment I looked at the injured man, that nothing could be done to save him, but the memory of the apparently uninterested drinkers, sitting watching and doing nothing in those circumstances, amazed me.

One Saturday morning after an Occasional Court of the Chairman of the Magistrates, Arthur Millward asked me if I would like to meet Sir Stanley Matthews as he was a friend calling on him for lunch. Stanley was en-route to Yorkshire as manager of Stoke City FC. I enjoyed my lunch chatting with such a marvellous footballer and a true gentleman.

I hadn't been in Heywood very long when the Licenced Victuallers invited us to what eventually became an annual dinner. I was asked to say a few words and I remarked that I had been given a lovely party before I left Rossendale. A voice at the back of the room said, "It wasn't half as good as the party the licensees had when they knew you had left." There was a howl of laughter which broke the ice completely. As a matter of fact, all licensees were aware that I didn't report anyone unless they had allowed drinking over an hour after the legal time limit.

Every Christmas Billy Green, a notorious burglar, was locked up. He was a rogue but never violent, just a pest and he was better off out of the way. Two years ago he stopped me on the street, shook my hand and asked me how I was!

The licensee and his wife of the New Inn at 'Owd Betts', close to the Rossendale boundary were extremely good to the police when there were serious accidents and snow storms on the moors. It was always a base for operations and coffee and biscuits were thrown in. Sadly, the elderly mother of the licensee was reported for allowing customers to drink five minutes after time on an occasion when I was on leave and an Inspector from Bury was covering the area. I was told that it broke her heart and she died soon afterwards.

One day, in deep snow, a troop of scouts went missing on the moors. This was in the time when policemen all had mobile phones. I asked for help and an Inspector with three constables joined me in a farmhouse at 'Owd Betts'. The farmer's wife told us we could use the farm as a base. I gave the Inspector the option of staying in the farmhouse warm and dry, or heading off the three miles or so towards Rochdale. Thankfully, he chose the snow and I had a cosy time in the farmhouse, warm and dry. The scouts were traced three hours later, safe and secure in a barn.

Opposite 'Owd Betts' there is a reservoir, and the waterworks house which was close by, was used as a polling booth. There were only sixteen people on the register, and only once did all sixteen vote. On a nice day the two polling officers used to sit out on the grass and when I joined them, the two deckchairs became three.

One of my constables, Sydney Ashburner was technically the Village Bobby for Ashworth Valley which included the hamlet of Ashworth, a few pubs and all the farms. He had the facility of a lightweight motor cycle. There wasn't enough work for him there, so he became the driver of the transit van. He told me that a landowner who resided at one of the farms had cut off the water supply to two neighbouring farms. Not a nice thing to do as it was also their domestic supply. I went to see them and resolved the conflict with a few words of advice to all three. A journalist, Stanley Browning was desperate to hear what had happened, but I didn't give him the news he wanted. Stanley, an ex-mayor of Heywood, always attended every court and also called in to the police station every morning. He was a reporter for the National Press and had the capacity for making the slightest information into a news story. He was a friend of mine, but one of his evening paper stories, I took exception to. En-route to the police station, a boy scout told him that the station Union Jack was flying upside down. We did put it right when he told us, but it had also gone to the Manchester Evening News. Sadly, he died suddenly in my presence at a Ball in 1965. He was a great chap and a good friend. His widow died fifty years later.

In the 1960's, during the notorious 'Moors Murders' which took place on Saddleworth Moor, we were informed that there was a grave on the hillside. I picked up two waterworks employees, one six feet tall and the other about five feet three inches and we set off across the rough ground towards Waugh's Well on the moors towards Edenfield. Eventually after about a mile, it became quite boggy and we had to leave the smaller chap behind. It was difficult jumping from dry patch to dry patch, but eventually we reached our destination. Some idiot had placed pebbles in the shape of a grave, but the only good thing about it all, was that I had discovered the place where Evelyn Waugh compiled his poetry overlooking the Rossendale valley which eventually led to the well being named after him.

The case of the Ghost Lorries

Harold Wright, a Rotarian friend lived in Arnold Avenue

off Manchester Road. He told me that motorway lorries which contained hard core for the new M62 were using Arnold Ave as a stopping place and number plates were being changed. I kept watch from his home and a couple of vehicles loaded with rocks stopped to change plates and others would stay half an hour then again leave with the loaded lorry.

I realised immediately that something sadly wrong was happening on the new M62 where access was in Birch Village a mile away and in reality it was multi scale theft. I used two of my policemen in plain clothes in an unmarked car who kept observations for two weeks. Also in that two week period I followed two different lorries to where the ballast in them was obtained. One was in Bacup and the other was in Edenfield. The Bacup picking up point used Irish drivers and the Edenfield one a Pakistani. Obtaining the Irish contingent's names was no problem, but the Pakistani's was a little more difficult.

I went to the Edenfield depot where the Pakistani manager decided he couldn't speak English, until I told him that his men would not be paid for any loads until I obtained the names of the men involved. Then he immediately decided to speak in perfect English and I left his office with full information.

As a result of this racket, thousands of tons of rock-fill, paid for by the main contractors, never reached the site. In the case of one of the haulage firms, the weight tickets signed by site checkers showed discrepancies of 4,000 tons. It was estimated that in total, 180,000 tons of rock had gone missing in three months. Registration numbers on delivery tickets had been 'borrowed' from the scrapped lorries of a Midlands firm. Lorries had been driven round and round the motorway check-point all day, delivering the same load up to five times. Eventually after a lengthy investigation, five men were prosecuted for the offences of forging false documents and dishonestly obtaining money. Each was fined, their combined fine being the sum of £1,125 and given a six months prison sentence, suspended for three years. This case became well publicised in the local press who coined the phrase 'Ghost Lorries'.

Clockwork Orange

Clockwork Orange was the name of an adult only film in 1973. There were no cinemas left in Heywood so the new Civic Centre showed films. The Town Council asked me to watch a preview of this film to see if it was fit to be shown in Heywood. I agreed that it was, but only to over 16's. In June that year, a rape was committed in Heywood and the Daily Mirror reported it as the 'Clockwork Orange Rape Hunt.' A 17 year old Dutch camper was raped in Ashworth Valley, while a 'Clockwork Orange' gang looked on. The girl's 20 year old boyfriend was held at knife point whilst she was raped. The gang were armed with clubs and wore black gloves with white stripes. The girl told police that the attack was similar to the one she had seen in the film 'Clockwork Orange'.

I was first at the scene of the rape and dogs were used, but they lost the scent. It was obvious to me that the youths had set off towards Bury, three miles away. I had obtained a very good description from the Dutch couple and I asked the Bury Inspector, Arthur Kemp to join me at the scene. Together we followed a path through the valley, along the lower slopes of the valley and through some thick woods. In the centre of the wood there was a cottage, and a middle aged lady came to the door. She hadn't seen anybody, but I asked her if she felt comfortable living alone in such surroundings, and she said, "I am safer here than in the centre of a city."

We carried on into the Fairfield Hospital part of Bury, and then abandoned our quest. Inspector Kemp passed all our information onto the Bury CID, and the descriptions were so good that the rapists were arrested the following day.

I had returned to Heywood Police Station where the young couple were being looked after and that evening I drove them to Windermere in my car as that was where they wanted to continue their camping holiday. I handed them over to the Cumbrian and Westmorland Police at Windermere with a request that their whereabouts be available if required. The youths pleaded guilty and received jail sentences. On my return to Heywood, I found a five pound note in my glove compartment!

The visit of George Brown, M.P.

In 1970, George Brown had applied for permission to hold an election meeting in Queen's Park in Heywood. His application was refused and he was extremely angry. He had strong words to say about the Town Clerk who had issued the refusal. Anxious Labour officials tried to restrain Mr Brown from starting the meeting in Queen's Park and eventually the meeting was held outside the gates. I was in the police station that day and was aware that Mr Brown had been refused this permission, and when I was notified that his gathering was holding up the traffic on Queen's Park Road, I took a police van with a driver and we went to Queen's Park Road. Traffic was waiting at both ends of the road and so I told him that if he didn't move I would arrest him for causing obstruction. The Daily Sketch carried the story on the following day and stated that I had been carrying my stick and asked Mr Brown to move on to prevent hold ups. Mr Brown was reported to have said to me, "Don't swing your stick so much son." I did wave my stick under his nose, but he moved into the park immediately, where he finished his meeting in the bandstand.

The Siege of Leopold Street

In November 1971 a gang of 4 men (3 of them IRA) carried out a Post Office raid in Manchester, and realising that their descriptions were known to the City Police, they rented a house in Leopold Street, Heywood. Leopold

Street was a narrow street of mainly terraced houses, running parallel to Manchester Road with Green Lane at its southern end. There were about thirty houses on each side of the street without any front gardens; however number 31, the house the gang had rented, was different in that it was detached from the rest. On either side of the house was a passage about four feet wide. The passages ran down the length of the house and ended at a brick wall that was the height of the building. It was possible to enter the kitchen of number 31 via a side door in the passage and there was also a window in this passage. In the other passage there was a bathroom window six feet off the ground.

The gang clearly intended to rent the property until the 'heat' was off and then make their escape. The four men, whose identities I will not reveal except to call them 'H', 'Sc', 'B', and 'Sm', along with two Irish women in their early twenties and two full grown Chow dogs, took up residence. In the following two weeks there was a significant increase in crime in the area around Leopold Street with shops and offices being burgled and a safe stolen from Hollinrake's office in the coal yard. All this activity was happening under the unsuspecting noses of the local CID, as opposite Leopold Street was the Hare and Hounds pub, a hostelry regularly frequented by the Detective Sergeant and his four detective constables.

A further crime was committed with the theft of a lorry overnight from West's Haulage Yard in a street off Manchester Road. The lorry was full of Boots Christmas merchandise. I circulated the details of the missing lorry to all the nearby forces and as a result we had our first slice of luck.

At six pm I received a phone call at home from D.C Hamer to inform me that a Superintendent from Leeds had rung but would only speak to the officer in charge. I returned his call and he informed me that they had found the lorry and the contents, and they had two prisoners in custody although three others had escaped. The situation at his end was quite complicated so I arranged to travel to Leeds to collect the prisoners.

The Boots Warehouse had a security officer, so I arranged for him, the manager from West's Haulage and two police officers to travel with me in our Police van to a Divisional Headquarters in the outer suburbs of Leeds. The plan I had in mind, was that Dick Berry, the Head of Security at Boots would sign for the recovered goods and Harry Mitchell, the manager from West's haulage would then drive the lorry and goods back to Heywood.

On arrival at Leeds there were a lot of detectives present in the building, more than I expected and I was quite impressed with the response from the Leeds division. However, having expressed how impressed I was with the turn out I was informed that it was nothing to do with the stolen lorry, but instead that one of the detectives was retiring and they were having a party for him, to which I was cordially invited to attend. I declined their generous offer.

I was directed to a room and found all the Boots merchandise strewn all over the floor. There was no way we were going to get that lot back to Heywood, so Harry Mitchell collected his lorry and drove it back to Heywood empty.

Once Harry was on his way I found out exactly what had happened. A man out walking his dog in a disused quarry on the outskirts of Leeds had noticed a lorry in the bottom of the quarry. Whilst he was watching, a small Hertz rental van arrived and parked up behind the lorry and two men proceeded to unload two pallets of goods from off the lorry and then drive away. The dog walker returned home and contacted the police. Within minutes of receiving this call the police HQ received a second call from a different part of the city from a householder who had witnessed two men unloading pallets of goods from a Hertz rental van and depositing them in a cottage opposite his house. He had then witnessed the men driving away with the empty pallets in the back of the van. The police operator realised that the two calls were connected and informed the two separate divisions of the information. A police car was directed towards the quarry and a raid was organised and carried out on the cottage.

The two police officers arrived at the quarry before the Hertz van and so they decided to hide their vehicle and sit inside the cab of the lorry. When the van arrived they let the two men start to throw the pallets into the back of the lorry and then hopped out and grabbed one each. Unfortunately one wriggled free and escaped, but they managed to apprehend the other one.

Things at the cottage didn't go to plan. The police entered simultaneously through the front and rear of the property but the two gang members jumped through the glass windows, receiving a number of injuries, but soon achieved their escape by running in opposite directions. The police did however arrest a fifth person who will be known as 'F', who as well as receiving stolen goods was also making illegal whiskey from his own still in the cottage. The Boots merchandise was recovered and taken to the police station that had recovered the lorry.

So at this point one member of the gang was in custody and the other three men had gone their own different ways, not aware of what has happened to each other with the exception of 'Sm' who knew that 'B' had been arrested. Presumably they had arranged that if things went wrong then they would make their separate ways back to the house on Leopold Street. At this time of course no one within the police knew that Leopold Street was where they were living.

Once I had found out the details of the afternoon's events I drove the police van to the police station where 'B' and 'F' were being held in order to take them back to Heywood and I was given permission by the desk sergeant to interview 'B'. I felt I needed to know as much about the gang as I could before returning to Heywood.

I managed to strike up a positive rapport quite quickly with him giving the impression that I knew more than I did and 'B' informed me that they were all living at 31 Leopold Street in Heywood. After half an hour he also informed me that he didn't want anyone to get killed. I think he said this because I had informed him that two men had escaped and he didn't want to be involved with any serious injuries which might be inflicted upon police officers. I assured him that anything he told me would be kept from the other gang members.

He informed me that he and two of the others were members of the IRA. 'S' wasn't; he was just a driver but the other two, 'Sc' and 'H' were the leaders of the gang. I was also informed that between them they had access to a double barrelled shotgun, a sawn off shot gun and a revolver with six bullets. Nowadays of course this would be handed over to an armed response team but this was in 1971 and I didn't have access to such a facility. Instead I informed the Leeds Police who returned to the cottage where they recovered the two shotguns.

I realised that I needed to get back to Heywood as quickly as I could, but before I set off I phoned the Heywood station and told the evening sergeant to round up as many officers as he possibly could including the two dog handlers, explaining that they should assemble at midnight in order to carry out a raid on a house.

At 11.30 I arrived back in Heywood with the two prisoners who were placed in separate cells. At midnight I had a detective sergeant, two detective constables, one sergeant, two police constables and two dog handlers. I gave them descriptions of the three men who had escaped in Leeds and informed them that there may be a loaded revolver in the premises. We parked our vehicles at the North end of Leopold Street and I took one of the detective constables with me to carry out a recce of the house.

Although the house was detached it did not have a garden and there was a light on in the downstairs front room. We approached the window and we could hear the voices of two women talking inside. We were about to check out the side passages when the piercing sound of a police whistle broke the silence. One of the other detectives had followed us down the street and he suddenly ran past us shouting, "He's there!" He had seen 'S' getting out of a car and so apprehended him before he could get away.

The two women had heard the commotion outside and opened the door, at which point I and D.C. Hamer entered the house and went into the front room. The two Chow dogs were about to attack us but the women held them back. I informed the women that I believed there were several men living in the premises but they denied this and said it was only them, but that there were some men living three doors down. Hamer went outside and I had a look around me. There was a staircase leading up to the upper floor and there was a door slightly ajar leading to the kitchen where there was a light on. I felt the presence of someone behind me and I turned to find Detective Inspector Mick Andrews from Bury. He had heard that there was an operation in progress and had arrived to help out. Arriving late, he had gone down the passage to one side of the house and had looked through the kitchen window. Whispering into my ear, he told me that he had seen someone in the kitchen. I crept into the kitchen, but it was empty. On my right was another door which led to the bathroom. It was closed, but cautiously I went to the door and opened it, and standing 4 feet away from me was 'H'. Pointing a revolver at my stomach he said, "If you come any closer I'll shoot." With my heart in my mouth I told him to put the gun down. I looked him in the face and saw a vicious man, whose face was disfigured by a scar running down the whole of one side. "I'll only get 10 years if I kill you," he grunted. The hand holding the gun was covered in blood and I believed he would shoot. I realised that if I grabbed the open bathroom door, I could close it between myself and the gunman and at least it would give me some protection. As I grabbed the door, he lunged at it to stop me from closing it. Fortunately Mick Andrews was on hand to help me pull the door shut and I grabbed a chair and jammed it under the handle to stop the door from being opened.

At this point Vic Swinney ran into the front room with Satan, the police dog. Vic slipped and fell and Satan went for the two Chows who clearly were more frightened than I was when I thought they were going to bite me! Vic regained control of Satan and things calmed down. It gave me a chance to appraise the situation. The gunman was locked in the bathroom, with Satan at the door anxious to get at him. The other dog handler was with Shane in the passage making sure that 'H' didn't climb through the window and we had enough men out in the street to deal with 'Sc' should he arrive. The question of course, was how we could get 'H' to come out without any trouble.

Using tear gas was a possibility and so I phoned Preston to speak to the Duty Inspector and explain what the situation was and ask for permission to use it. Permission was granted on the understanding that I evacuated all the houses in the street first. This would take too long, so tear gas was out of the question.

I asked him if I could let one of the dogs loose in the bathroom to get the gunman but he refused, saying that if it was shot, it would cost £2000 to replace a highly trained police dog. I wondered whether a policeman's life was cheaper but didn't say anything.

In those days there were no armed response teams available and so the only thing we could do was wait and see if 'H' got fed up enough to give himself up or come out shooting. By now the excitement had drawn a lot of officers from across the force and the house was getting quite crowded. The two women had been shunted upstairs to the front bedroom with the two dogs. The Chief Superintendent from Bury had arrived, closely followed by the Detective Superintendent and then the Assistant Chief Constable. I decided to take a back seat and let them make the decisions. In the bathroom, the gunman wasn't making a sound, and this siege situation lasted for three hours.

The Chief Superintendent said that we needed a gun.

One of the constables said he knew someone who had a gun so he left, returning a short time later with a shotgun. I didn't ask where he got it from but I assumed that he had knocked up a local farmer at 2 am and asked him for his gun. It's hard to imagine that this is what the police had to do if they were confronted with an armed criminal but things were different in those days.

The Chief Superintendent shouted through the bathroom door informing 'H' that the police too had a gun and if he didn't bloody well come out he'd shoot him. I was in the front room thinking, well there are three senior officers in there; if they get shot it won't be my fault! My thoughts were interrupted by someone saying that we needed a blanket because if a bullet hits a loosely held blanket it would absorb the force of the bullet and it would just drop. This had to be a crackpot idea surely.

There was a lot of shouting and chattering going on both inside and outside the house but there was still silence in the bathroom. Time was moving on and I started to become concerned that 'H' may have managed to escape. I knew he couldn't get out through the door, window or ceiling but what about a cellar; maybe he could get out from under the house, but with so many police outside there was no way he could make his escape.

After three hours 'H' gave himself up. He was told to leave the gun in the bathroom and to come out which he did, and was very forcefully arrested. His first words were, "it isn't a real gun." He was arrested and taken away by CID and I sent my staff away with the exception of one PC who was in charge of the two women.

The three senior officers, the Detective Inspector and I remained at the premises. Firstly I retrieved the gun which had been left on a bathroom cabinet next to Hollinrake's broken safe. On examination, I knew that it was no longer a gun that could be fired. In the three hours silence, 'H' had found a metal comb, removed the cylinder from the gun and very astutely fashioned the comb to make it look like the cylinder and make the gun into a replica. However

I knew that the gun I had seen was the real thing and so carried out a search of the bathroom. In the toilet cistern I found the cylinder but was unable to locate the six bullets. Later that morning, having racked my brains as to where the bullets could possibly be, I returned to the house and climbed on a chair in the bathroom and felt in the window recess at the bottom of the window. Between the glass and the wood there was a narrow gap and the bullets were all lined up one behind the other.

Well we had 'H', but 'Sc' was still on the loose. The house was placed under twenty-four hour surveillance and two constables in an unmarked car were ordered to follow the two women if they left the house, especially if they took the dogs with them, as we knew that 'Sc' loved the animals. The next day a Manchester taxi arrived at the house, and the women with the two dogs got in and drove off. They were followed as far as Cheetham Hill, where the police car was boxed in at some traffic lights and so they lost the taxi. Fortunately they had the taxi license number and the firm was contacted. They informed us that the two women and the dogs had been dropped off on a busy street in Blackley.

I contacted Manchester City Police and gave them a description of the final IRA member still at large, and asked that they be on the lookout for him and arrest him on sight. I also gave details of the two women and suggested that, if seen, they were followed as they could lead us to wherever 'Sc' was living. The Manchester Police obviously complied with my request as he was arrested by a woman PC. In her statement she said, "I saw a man fitting his description walking two Chow dogs. As I approached him he started to run. I swung my handbag at him and inside was a rather heavy mobile radio. 'Sc' lost his balance, fell and struck his head on the edge of the pavement which knocked him out." As a result, he was arrested and delivered to us at Heywood.

I now had five men in custody but only four cells and although each cell could take two prisoners, I wanted to keep all the men separate. I got permission to release on bail the man who had received the stolen goods. He was not part of the gang, had an infection in his toes and fingers and was not at risk of absconding. This man never appeared in court as he died before his case was brought to trial.

'H' boasted that the IRA would come for them and in fact he did attempt to escape from the cell via an air vent in the ceiling but having swung himself up on top of a cupboard he discovered that the vent was only big enough for his head to fit through. I arranged for an Occasional Court session and all four were transferred to Strangeways Prison to await Quarter Sessions for judgement. They all received jail sentences.

'B' had undoubtedly provided us with really good information and quite possibly saved my life by mentioning the guns. I wanted to speak to the judge about taking into account his statement but 'B' didn't want this because he was scared that they would kill him. In the two weeks following the incident I lost two stones in weight, as clearly the stress of the whole affair had affected me.

There is a post script to this story. Ten years later, the Methodist Church, which was close to the house in Leopold St and had been unused for many years, was being demolished. Whilst driving past I looked across to where the back wall was still standing and I noticed the outlines of a doorway. I stopped and went over to take a closer look and found that the inside of the doorway was only plaster and realised that it was actually a connecting wall with 31 Leopold Street and behind this plaster doorway was the bathroom where the siege had taken place! Had 'H' known that there was only a thin layer of plaster between him and escape, the ending to this story could have been quite different!

Kidnap trauma for Pools winner

In May 1975, whilst I was based at Radcliffe, five year old

Vanessa Carr was snatched from outside her school. Only two weeks previously, her father, Danny Carr had won £500,000 on the Pools, probably the equivalent of £4.5 million today. A Whitefield chip shop owner had read about Danny's win in the press and subsequently kidnapped his daughter making several ransom demands. Most of the available police officers were being deployed to man phone kiosks in the area because they were following a lead that the kidnapper would ring from one of them. However, the CID had neglected to question the residents close to the school where Vanessa had attended to see if anyone had seen anything, so I sent a young copper to do that and within twenty minutes he had found a neighbour who had been smoking in his garden when he saw a young girl get into a car in the school yard. He had written the car registration number on his cigarette packet which eventually led us to the kidnapper.

The car had been stolen and after a police chase, the vehicle was recovered in the Langworthy area of Salford, with Vanessa inside and unharmed. It is highly likely that we saved her life, because it is most unlikely for a kidnapper to save the life of his victim if they have seen both their attacker and where they live. The man who had kidnapped Vanessa was sentenced to twelve years in prison. It must have been the shortest kidnap in history and a rare occurrence to recover the victim in less than three hours.

Almost forty years after this event, in 2013, I met up with Danny Carr at Hopwood Unionist Club. After the kidnapping, Danny moved to Spain where he lived for many years. He has since moved back to Lancashire, but Vanessa still lives in Spain. The reunion was quite emotional and Danny kept on shaking my hand as he told me that he knew I had saved his daughter's life. It was lovely to meet him again and piece together the details of the story.

Frightened ?

Since retiring from the police in 1977 after 31 years' service, I have spoken about life as a policeman to children on a number of occasions. They would often ask if I had ever been afraid or had I ever seen a ghost. The answer to the first question is yes to the second no.

The most eerie places are old buildings, especially when the wind is blowing and it is in the dead of night. It can be absolutely silent but suddenly you will hear the creaking of water pipes or the rustling of curtains and you swing your torch around but there is nothing to see.

In the early 1950s at 2am I went to Clitheroe Castle to check that a building used by the Town Council was secure. Earlier in the evening I had been to the cinema and watched a film in which seven policemen walking alone had been stabbed and killed. After checking and finding the building secure I was standing at the top of a flight of stone steps looking down over the town which was calm and peaceful. To my side was a large chestnut tree with its lowest branches probably about 3 feet above my head. Suddenly behind me I heard a slight rustling noise and a white barn owl flew right over my head in the gap between the branch and my helmet and just as it passed it let out a long screech. I literally jumped a foot in the air. Was I frightened? Absolutely! Had it screeched a second earlier, it would probably have collided with me! Talk about being frightened to death!

Ghostly appearances

I have only been involved in two incidents relating to the appearance of ghosts. I personally don't believe in ghosts but I'm sure that people who do are genuine in their beliefs and there is no way of changing their minds about what they saw.

In 1976 I was at Prestwich and one of the constables asked if he could transfer from one police house into another. They had a young daughter and when they put her to bed they would shortly after hear her talking to someone. Each time they went to investigate, they had seen another small girl sitting on the bottom of their daughter's bed and when they entered the room the girl disappeared.

There was no record of the previous occupants having seen a ghost, but by mutual consent they were able to exchange homes with another couple who never reported seeing a ghost and like most ghost stories it remains a mystery.

The second story was when I moved office in 1985 from the Boots warehouse on Pilsworth Estate to the large warehouse in Heywood. I was told that the first floor of the oldest part of the mill had a ghost. I stayed in that office for three years and never saw an apparition. A lady ghost had been seen at different times during the past 100 years, and only in that room; however one of the warehouse security guards said he had seen it twice at night and there was no way he would enter the room on his own. So as far as some people are concerned this peaceful lady is at least 100 years old and still wandering around.

The Disappearance of Martha Hardy

By all accounts, Martha Hardy was an eccentric woman. In 1963, at the age of seventy four she was a sturdy woman with tightly curled white hair, about five feet three inches tall and a wealthy heiress. She had been left £10,000 by her brother that was deposited in the Halifax Building Society; as well as a further £20,000 by her husband who had died some thirteen years previously. Martha's relationship with her neighbours in Starkey Street was said to have been rather awkward, having occasionally sent them solicitor's letters to settle whatever un-resolved disagreements she might have had. One exception to this was Lillian Nuttall, her next door neighbour, who was a beneficiary in Martha's Will and was to receive her house after Martha's death. A careful woman, Martha was not known to leave the house after dark, and she was always conscious of her home security.

After the death of her husband, Martha struck up a friendship with Wilfred Holt, an estate agent who had his offices in Central Chambers above shops at 6-10 Market Place, Heywood. Mr Holt also ran the local Halifax Building Society Agency from his premises at Central Chambers. The offices of a solicitor and an accountant were also above the shops in Market Place; one of which was a butcher's owned by Mr and Mrs Clegg. It is quite probable that Wilfred Holt had a set of duplicate keys to both of the cellars of Central Chambers as well as numbers 8 and 10 Market place. In theory, this could allow him access to these premises at any time. Wilfred Holt played a large part in Martha's life and she visited his offices most days. In this respect, she was a creature of habit.

Martha must have enjoyed the company of this man as she had changed her will several times in the few years before her disappearance, making Wilfred Holt the executor and principal beneficiary, a fact that he later said he knew nothing about. Family disagreements meant that Martha had disinherited her daughter some time previously and Jane Brassington, Martha's sister, had left Martha out of her will too. Ultimately, money seemed to be at the heart of this case.

Martha's sister, Miss Jane Brassington lived in Stretford. Jane had been friendly with a man who can be referred to as WF. He often did plumbing jobs for her as well as being a part time taxi driver. This man was to play a major role in the mystery which unfolded.

On the 19th November 1963, Miss Brassington was found by this friend to be suffering from coal gas poisoning and was subsequently rushed to hospital in Davyhulme, where she was admitted. Martha decided to go and visit her sister in hospital that same day and was taken by local taxi driver, George Ribchester. When she arrived at the hospital, she was asked by staff to return the following day when Miss Brassington would be fit enough to see her and so she returned home.

The following day, at about 2.30pm, Martha spoke to Mrs Clegg, wife of the butcher and told her that she was going to see her sister in hospital. She also asked Mrs Clegg to pass on this information to Mr Holt and let him know that she would see him later. Mrs Clegg did as she had been asked and the information was passed on to Mr Holt's office girl and Martha set off once more to see her sister; this time in a taxi driven by Miss Brassington's friend, WF. Later, in questioning, he told police that he had taken her to the hospital to see Miss Brassington, and then taken her back to her sister's house in Stretford, where he left her. The hospital had no record of Martha's visit and she was never seen again.

Several unexplained things happened. The Cleggs had been in the habit of burning offal, but on one occasion, not long after Martha's disappearance and before she had been reported missing, Mr Holt complained that he was getting smoked out of his office by the smell of burning offal. In response, the Cleggs discontinued this practise. At about the same time, an unexplained pile of new sand was found in the Clegg's cellar which was a mystery to them having thought that they were the only ones who had a key and therefore the only ones with access to the cellar.

In spite of the fact that Wilfred Holt had been told that Martha was planning to visit him later in the day of the 20th November, he failed to report her missing until many days later. Before he decided to go and report her disappearance, he apparently told his wife that a woman from Heywood was missing, and that he knew her. He waited until the 2nd of December before he went to the police and told them that he thought Martha had gone missing, and police enquiries commenced. A further lull in the investigation then commenced as police followed the lead that Martha, following her previously stated intention, may have gone to America to visit her daughter there. This became a 'wild goose chase' and only added unproductive time to the investigation as no trace of her was ever found in the U.S.

Martha's home in 79 Starkey Street was searched and no evidence of criminal action was found, although by the end of January 1964 a nationwide appeal had been launched which mentioned the possibility of 'foul play'. Indeed, no photographs of the missing woman could be found, making the appeal quite difficult and Martha became one of the thousands of people classed as 'missing from home'. A search of Miss Brassington's home was also undertaken and no trace of Martha could be found.

Several suspects were questioned. The taxi driver, WF, was questioned about his contact with Martha, as from his statement it was obvious that his was the last ever sighting of her alive. He told the police that after their short visit to the hospital on the 20th November, he had dropped Mrs Hardy at her sister's home. Sightings of WF had also been made outside 79 Starkey St as he called at Mrs Hardy's home on November 26th. Why?

Mr Holt also came under scrutiny but on questioning, he passed any traces of suspicion towards the taxi driver WF, saying that this man had been in Miss Brassington's will and that he could easily have disposed of a body in Stretford. Police then turned their enquiries in the direction of Stretford, again with no result. In early December 1963, a letter from Miss Brassington was opened by Mr Holt's clerk, which accused him of 'getting rid of my sister'. Mr Holt instructed his clerk to burn the letter and to keep its existence a secret. In a conversation with Mr Holt, Eric Clegg was reported to have commented that people were saying Martha had been murdered. Mr Holt appeared to be puzzled by his remarks and replied, "Why do you say that?"

A third suspect who had been a friend of Mrs Hardy was interviewed. Fred Flewker was a local barber whom Martha often visited on his allotment off Starkey St, returning with fresh vegetables. Repeated police questioning apparently made him ill.

By February 1964, police enquiries had discovered that Wilfred Holt's financial situation was in dire straits. An I.O.U. was found among Mrs Hardy's papers showing that Mr Holt had borrowed money from her. Later enquiries discovered that he had misappropriated funds from the Halifax Building Society Agency which he also ran from his office in Central Chambers and he was eventually prosecuted but given a suspended sentence. By the end of 1964, it had become apparent that Wilfred Holt had been the beneficiary in the wills of several other elderly people. Knowing that he was a beneficiary in Martha's will, it was obvious that his financial situation would be much improved on the event of her death.

In February 1964, Martha Hardy's daughter, Mrs Burton arrived in England with her husband from Canada to pursue the case herself. On visiting her mother's house, she found some items missing, including a brown leather case which was later seen in Mr Holt's office. By this time, it was now known that Wilfred Holt had a previous conviction for embezzlement and the plot thickened. Martha's brown leather handbag which contained her pension book was never found and there was no attempt to cash in her weekly pension after she disappeared. Mrs Burton was determined to stay in England for as long as it took to clear up the mystery of her mother's whereabouts. After talking to the police, Mrs Burton was convinced that her mother had been murdered and that false statements had been made. An artist's impression of Martha Hardy was duly issued by the police in an effort to trace her, but Mrs Burton was considering hiring a private detective to help them with the case as the Lancashire Murder Squad had decided that no evidence of foul play could be found and so the case was classed as 'missing from home'.

The police drawing of Martha Hardy

In May 1964, Jane Brassington was found dead in her home by her taxi driver friend WF. She had a double fracture of the jaw and serious head wounds which could only have been caused by a severe blow to the head or a very heavy fall. The inquest did not determine what the cause of death was although it is said that she died of a brain haemorrhage, and the Coroner recorded Miss Brassington's death an 'open verdict'. £2000 was missing from her bank account and police interviewed the taxi driver, requesting from him a sample of his handwriting which he refused to give. If a man is innocent, it is bound to increase suspicion when he does not assist the police with their enquiries, but the sample of handwriting was never given. However, within his judgements, the coroner had exonerated WF and so other questioning was of no avail.

Although Miss Brassington had made a will, it was in favour of a sister in Australia who had predeceased her and so in effect, she died intestate. Her estate was subsequently divided between different branches of the family. Another riddle added to the deaths of the two sisters; there had been withdrawals from Miss Brassington's building Society account which were never traced. During August 1964, two withdrawals were made authorising a 'J. Dean' to receive £200 and £195. Detectives discovered that it was a fictitious name and address which had been given.

Gradually the search for Martha slowed down as a lack of evidence made proving any suspicions difficult. It became a yearly reminder in the local press when the case would be resurrected once more. The Bridgewater Canal was searched by the Lancashire Police Underwater team and a clairvoyant from Scandinavia was hired by Mrs Burton who dressed as her mother in a reconstruction; all to no avail. A reward of £1000 was issued by Mrs Burton for information about her mother. A brief flurry of activity brought the case to the forefront at the end of December 1965 when a man claimed that Martha Hardy had been murdered, her body put into a drum which was then filled with cement and deposited in a corporation tip in Stretford. Insinuations were also made that her body had been hidden somewhere in or around Central Chambers, 8/10 Market Place, Heywood. Nothing was proved of either of these suggestions. The case slowed down and Mrs Burton returned to Canada, leaving with the conviction that her mother had been murdered.

Wilfred Holt was in serious financial difficulties and his business began to dwindle. In 1966, along with Mr Clegg, he began proceedings to sell 8/10 Market Place to a property company. He was reluctant in the end to sign the contract and we can only speculate as to why, but on 31st March 1967, just before the contract was due to be signed, Wilfred Holt died owing approximately £12,000. It might appear that he did not really wish to dispose of the property and in fact did not sign the contract. By 1970, it was fast becoming the time when Martha could be declared legally dead and her assets, which up until now had been frozen, could be dealt with. Martha's daughter, Mrs Burton, was shocked to find that that her mother's will had been changed twice and that Wilfred Holt, now deceased, was now the main beneficiary. Mrs Holt was going to court to fight the case as she claimed that she needed the money.

Throughout the early stages of this case, a solitary Detective Constable had been put in charge of enquiries. Nine years after Martha's disappearance, I got the opportunity I had been waiting for to pursue the case myself. Mr Thornton, a friend who had recently retired, had been Martha's accountant with an office in Central Chambers alongside the Estate Agents. Mr Thornton had dealt with Martha's taxation matters and so using information that he had previously been unable to recount, he told me that when Lancashire Murder Squad had become involved, they had dug up the wrong cellar.

I rang Headquarters at Preston and asked them to send me the Martha Hardy file, which they did. During the next fortnight, I meticulously examined the contents and copied anything of interest with special attention to the names of the people who had been interviewed. Whilst the file was in my possession, I realised that mistakes had been made in the process of the initial enquiry. Police had initially presumed that Martha was just missing from home after visiting her sister in Stretford and it was not until much later that the real possibility of foul play became evident. I have still retained the notes I made, along with the accountants typewritten account of what he knew. I sent a copy of the letter to HQ when I returned the file. Subsequently, I re-interviewed everyone who was still alive and the most useful witness was Mrs Clegg who informed me about the conversation she had had with Martha on the day she died. When interviewed, she also told me about the letter that Holt's clerk had opened from

Miss Brassington accusing him of getting rid of her sister. The incident of the burning offal was described in detail as they had been told that under no circumstances must they burn offal again. Lastly, she described the new pile of sand which she had discovered in their cellar. Whether or not these snippets of information had been given previously to police, I do not know.

I returned the files with a request to enter the appropriate premises for the purpose of digging up the cellar. This permission was granted, but I was told that the Murder Squad Superintendent at that time would also be present. He arrived and along with two men to do the digging, we entered the cellar. To my disbelief, the Superintendent then produced a divining rod and a scornful comment from me saying that we weren't there to find water, didn't go down well. In reply he told me that his divining rod found dead bodies! No dead bodies were found, but we noticed that one stone flag was loose. Beneath it was new sand. Digging down several feet below the flag produced no result, but the full page newspaper headline that ensued read; 'Missing Martha: Police deny 'new dig' move'. The Advertiser recount which followed that headline reported: 'Police and a local solicitor have denied any knowledge of a will being discovered which pinpoints the spot where the body of Martha Hardy can be found'... 'Chief Inspector John Wilson said no digging had taken place in the basement of shops in Market Place or anywhere else and "No body had been found." I never actually denied the dig, but I did tell the Press that I knew nothing about the contents of her will.

Martha was officially declared dead in an announcement on 12 Dec 1974. Margaret Burton had asked the High Court for the declaration and that she be the main beneficiary in her mother's will; but there was still doubt as to who would inherit. Letters of Administration had been issued and were with a Rochdale solicitor. Eventually, the proceeds from the will were split between Mrs Burton and the widow of Wilfred Holt.

As the years have passed by since this unsolved mystery, the buildings which held Central Chambers have long since been demolished and any evidence which lay hidden there disappeared in the rubble. The files which the police held have been destroyed as it was never classed as a murder case and indeed, the only evidence that I know of with the exception of newspaper archives is still in my possession: the notes which I made, and the typewritten evidence given to me by my friend Mr Thornton.

In my opinion, it is this written testimony which points the finger at both the taxi driver and a person whom she considered a friend, as the perpetrators of the crime. Martha's clothing could have been burnt in the cellar, causing the blockage in the chimney that resulted in the office above the butchers shop being smoky. Some belief at the time was that her body had been put in a drum and buried. Had that been so it would have been deposited in Heywood tip as it was open to vehicles both day and night. I later found that a man fitting the name and description of the taxi driver had purchased an oil drum and cement from a firm in Bury.

My theory of events is this; Martha would have been with the taxi driver throughout the afternoon. After the shops were closed at 5pm, she would have walked with the driver up the very dark back street to her death. Her body was dismembered in the cellar of the butcher's shop and then ten days elapsed before she was reported missing by her friend who had keys to all three premises. All the instruments required were in the butcher's shop. In the 1970's, Heywood tip became a housing estate and so I don't expect her body will ever be found.

There were other possible disposal sites: the lake in the local park, although this is quite shallow and difficult to access as the gates are closed at night, and a lodge within the Mutual Mills complex which was very deep, but again there would have been twenty four hour security on the site. Perhaps what was needed at the time to solve this mystery was a police double act; not unlike the ones we now see on television.

Whitefield

In 1974, Heywood became part of Rochdale and Rochdale as a division was amalgamated into Greater Manchester Police. As a Chief Inspector in Lancashire, I was offered a post which would be somewhere in Lancashire, possibly Accrington, Rossendale or Burnley, but I chose to move into the city force and so stay at Jesmond Dene. The town police station became part of the sub division of Rochdale and I was transferred to Whitefield Sub Division which comprised the three townships of Whitefield, Radcliffe and Prestwich, (still part of Bury Division). It was a case of moving my pictures from my office in Heywood Police Station and fitting into a much smaller office in Whitefield. Policemen were moving around in all directions.

A few weeks after moving, my very good friend and neighbour, Herbert Bold, died. I knew that St Luke's Church in Heywood would be filled to capacity at his funeral service and so I called at Heywood enquiry office to advise them that there would be a lot of cars at the funeral service in St Luke's. The senior constable I spoke to asked me where the church was, and given that it was only fifty yards away in the town centre, I was dismayed. I could see all we had worked for during the previous ten years 'going to pot.' My next visit to the police station in Heywood was after I retired three years later.

I became second in command of Whitefield Sub Division based in Whitefield Police Station, a brand new police station opposite Stand Parish Church. The Superintendent John Eccles had been a friend for several years. He ran as it was, a 'happy ship' and there were four other inspectors, and nine sergeants in that sub division as well as a policewoman sergeant. I had some very mixed feelings and knew that I wasn't happy. There was nothing wrong with the bobbies, but I had returned to a city force where after an eight hour shift, you returned home.

It was five miles from my home, down the M62 motorway to Whitefield and I would arrive at 8 am. As usual I would read all the telephone messages, and then deal with the correspondence and reports. When I had finished the correspondence, I virtually had the sub division to wander round. Sometimes I walked down to Radcliffe, then the four miles through the streets to Prestwich and finish back in Whitefield. It passed the time on. If the inspectors and sergeants had any problems to solve, then I would help later.

There could be twenty traffic accidents a day on the five mile Whitefield stretch of the motorway, due to numerous accidents in 'Death Valley'. A large number occurred at night as at that time the motorway was unlit and heavy duty vehicles were allowed to use all three lanes. Greater Manchester Police were inundated with complaints and several Superintendents were dealing with them, one of whom was John Eccles, so I rarely saw him. I was once talking to a nice young bobby who had come in for petrol and five minutes after he left the station, he collided with the back of a lorry loaded with trees as he was driving up the slip road onto the motorway, and was killed; a very sad accident.

Most of Heaton Park is situated in Prestwich and owned by Manchester City Council. It was decided to have a large bonfire on the top side, close to Prestwich Railway Station and the main road from Bessies 'O' the Barn to Cheetham Hill. I was invited to a meeting at Prestwich Police Station presided over by a Manchester City Police Detective Superintendent.

I listened to him talking about 1000 cars and thousands of pedestrians going to this bonfire at about 6pm at night, through one entrance gate. I asked him who was going to do the traffic duty to keep thousands of people safe and he told me that it would be the beat constables. In reply, I told him that it was a stupid idea, that it was too dangerous and that none of my bobbies were going to stand in the middle of a main road at peak time trying to get people into a park. The scheme was abandoned but I got some dirty looks from the Superintendent!

Prestwich Mental Hospital

One source of trouble was Prestwich Mental Hospital. I was asked to deal with everything that occurred there; unusual deaths, missing people, disturbances etc. There were numerous wards and outbuildings, fields, woods, sewerage pits and swamps, as well as a large area of rough terrain at the rear between the hospital and the River Irwell which was the hospital boundary. I made a plan of the site which enabled each block to be searched diligently. It meant that I was called out from home quite often. The police horses, dogs and underwater team became involved. If police were searching, they always got a meal in the hospital canteen. On one occasion, there was a search for a missing female patient who was known by everyone at the hospital, not by name, but because she only ever spoke two words; 'piss off'. I had the Mounted Police, police dogs and we searched for two full days without finding her. One nurse said that she had seen her walking towards the back of the hospital and she was given the usual two words. We spent most of our time investigating and searching the rear of the hospital, but about a year later, when I was at Prestwich Police Ball in evening dress, I was told that she had been found. She had been within five yards of the front gate on the main road. At the time of her death there had been an abundance of prickly blackberry bushes in full bloom and she had obviously crawled behind them and up against the wall of a bungalow where she died. Her skeleton was found complete with a woollen hat, dress and shoes. On the bungalow side of the wall, there had been a manure heap. Whilst we had initially been searching, the police dogs would not go into the prickly bushes, and any smell emitting from the body would have co-existed with the smell of the manure heap. This had obviously hindered our search and one of the reasons for

168

not finding her body as quickly as we could have.

Much of what I saw at Prestwich hospital saddened me and the incidents that occurred became commonplace. A lady would sit knitting constantly and her garment never grew as every two rows or so she would pull it all out and start again. We were once called out to an inmate from the hospital, who had climbed up one of the electricity pylons which ran through the grounds of the hospital. Fortunately for him, one of the six cables at the top of the pylon was not working otherwise he would have been killed instantly. He climbed to the top and just sat there. Onlookers glanced nervously up and we were called, along with the fire brigade to see if we could coax him down. The risk to officers was too great for me to send one of my P.C's climbing up there to rescue him and the fire brigade also relinquished any responsibility so we watched and waited. Eventually he climbed down of his own accord, unhurt and none the worse for his escapade, but this was the sort of incident the inmates were involved in.

I had a very interesting time with a film crew who were filming a ghost story in the woods at the rear of the hospital. One of the stars of Last of the Summer Wine, Peter Sallis, was the main character and I had lunch with them in their touring cafeteria. They had erected a castle and they were going to leave the site unguarded until I told them that they required a couple of security guards overnight. Otherwise all their property would disappear. I knew that two of the hospital male nurses who would be willing to earn a few pounds pocket money, which solved their problem. For some reason, the story they were filming never made it to the television screen.

Murder in Radcliffe

A couple in their thirties who lived on Darnhill, had always caused me some consternation. They were involved in several different traffic offences which the wife always admitted to and pleaded guilty, although we had always suspected that the husband had committed the offences. They moved to Radcliffe. One day we were called to a murder and it was this couple who were involved. When we arrived at the scene, the house was covered in blood. The wife had got so fed up with her husband blaming her that she waited for him to fall asleep in his bed and then smashed his head with a coal hammer. This first blow had probably killed him, but to make sure that he was indeed dead, she continued to deluge blow after blow onto his head until it was pulp. In spite of the murder charge, she only served a short sentence in prison, as they had taken into consideration her many years of anguish at the hands of her husband.

Prestwich has a large Jewish population and the next two cases are good illustrations of how their attendance to Sabbath rules could affect the outcome of incidents in the area.

Treasure!

An interesting and unusual incident arose at the Jewish School in Prestwich. The driver of a bulldozer was excavating ground for a new school yard when he noticed numerous pieces of tin about the size of a ten pence piece, which had fallen out of a clay jar. Children were playing about and he gave them some pieces of the tin, some whole, some halves and quarters; but kept some for himself.

This had happened the day before the Jewish Sabbath and one of the boys who had received the tin pieces, lived in Stockport. He showed them to his father who took them to a jewellers shop to see if they were valuable. A customer in the shop said that he would give them £200 for the six bits of tin. They kept what they now knew to be coins, and informed Prestwich Police Station. They were actually King Stephen pennies, half pennies and quarter pennies. Whilst this was happening in Stockport, the school caretaker, who had also been given some of the coins, was doing quite a lot of digging on his own. He had full access and as it was now the Sabbath, the School authorities were helpless. At this point, I was dealing with treasure trove and eventually I had a minimum value of around £2000 worth of coins which I handed in to Bury headquarters to be placed in the safe.

The British Museum took possession of the coins which were of tremendous value, and the bulldozer driver and the school caretaker became very rich men. A year later, the sergeant at Prestwich retired and emigrated to New Zealand where some time later some of the coins turned up. The museum said that they thought a rich man had buried the coins under a tree then went off to fight in the Civil War, but never returned to claim his treasure.

Stolen pram

On another occasion a Jewish lady complained that her pram had been stolen. I took the details from her and quickly realised that she knew the exact time of the theft. When I asked her how she was so sure of the time the pram was stolen, she said that she had seen the incident. I was amazed that having watched the pram being taken, she didn't actually do anything to get it back immediately so I quizzed her about her motives. She explained that as it was the Jewish Sabbath, and so she wasn't allowed to do this. I explained in reply that if she wasn't prepared to go after the pram and the thief when she had seen the incident, then I wasn't prepared to send one of my bobbies to find it. She left rather disgruntled, and I don't know if her pram was ever found or not.

The ghostly voice

The verger at Stand Paris Church once told me that a crypt had been broken into in the church graveyard. There was a hole alongside the grave. I asked a young P.C. who was with me to slide down into the crypt and it was found that two large coffins and a baby coffin had been opened. It started to drizzle and I was getting soaked to the skin, so I radioed in to ask if someone could bring my raincoat down to the churchyard. A young policewoman arrived soon after and just as she was handing it to me, a voice from below the ground said, "I don't like it down here!" Her face went white with the shock and she dropped my coat and she would have collapsed had I not grabbed her. The young P.C. then climbed from his hiding place under the ground and the owner of the ghostly voice was revealed.

Promotion or retirement?

In 1977, Chief Inspector Tomlinson informed me that there was a vacancy for a Superintendent in 'A' Division, the city centre, and that he had recommended me for the position. Obviously there was a short list and four Chief Inspectors appeared before a panel at H.Q. The Chief Constable, Deputy and one other; none of whom I had met in the three years as Chief Inspector, were the selection panel. Two of the other candidates I didn't know, but the third was the officer in charge of the Manchester City Training School at Sedgley Park. I knew from that moment that it was a set up. There would be one winner and it wouldn't be the three unknowns.

My interview didn't last long. I was asked where I had served, and then came a crucial question: "What do you think of the Manchester Police?"

My reply was, "If I had wanted to join them, I would have done so thirty years ago." I thanked them and three solemn faces looked at me as I walked out. When I retired a couple of months later, I was asked if I wished to say goodbye at H.Q. I declined. I already knew that a job was being created for me at Boots Chemists and that Nan would be able to travel round with me.

Boots 1977

In 1964 when I arrived in Heywood, I visited the Boots warehouse in Taylor Street to meet the manager Alfred Oakes, and his deputy Leslie Hindmarch. It had been a very old cotton mill which was supposed to have been haunted and was the cosmetics, drugs and medicines warehouse for the whole of Northern England and Scotland. Mr Oakes was a rotund, jovial, little man, but the mainstay of the premises was Leslie Hindmarch who had been a chemist during the war years. He had married Eileen, a lovely Irish lady and came up to Heywood, taking up residence in Prestwich. Les and I became instant friends. They had four grandsons; Richard, Robin, Robert and Roger who called me Uncle Jack.

The warehouse was situated in a very congested area of the town. Two of the four streets surrounding it were quite narrow and it was frequently congested, the volume of traffic causing obstruction. I was asked by Mr Oakes if I could accompany him to see if he could rent additional warehouse accommodation. He would ideally have liked premises near the old mill but that was impossible so it was decided that the next best place would be a new building on the Pilsworth Industrial Estate. This became the distribution depot.

One of the narrow streets near the mill was Hill Street. It was used as an incoming dock entrance, but this meant that every lorry delivering goods blocked the street as it backed into the premises. There was some spare ground opposite the entrance which I asked Boots to tarmac. This enabled cars to continue their journey without any hold up. The other narrow street, which also had an unloading dock, also held the warehouse premises for a furniture and television dealer, James Beddoes, who had four large shops in the Rochdale and Bury area. Jim Beddoes was a friend of mine in the Rotary Club, but when I asked him to leave his lorry inside his yard he insisted that he had as much right as Boots had to use the street. He was referring to his empty van which was parked outside his office. I told him that I would have yellow lines placed along the street if he didn't behave. The yellow lines were put in place which stopped the aggravation. It served him right.... but ended the friendship.

Twice a week I had coffee and biscuits with the two bosses in the large office block. The receptionist and telephone operator Hazel has been a friend for fifty years. I met all the top managers of Boots from Nottingham including the Chief Security Officer who had been a Detective Chief Superintendent in Nottingham. He always called on me for a chat and coffee. The new breathalyser kit was introduced to all the police forces and this coincided with the Annual Boots Drivers' awards, so I was invited to present their awards, then tell them about the breathalyser which I tested on some of them.

In the late 1970's, Boots realised that losses in the transportation of goods throughout the UK was tremendous so their Chief Security Officer organised a transit security department. There were to be ten areas, each covered by a transit security officer, all ex-police officers. Knowing I was about to retire, I was asked if I would like the North West area which stretched from Newtown in Mid Wales, west of the Pennines through North Wales, Cheshire, Wirral, part of Derbyshire, Greater Manchester, Merseyside, Lancashire and Cumbria up to the Scottish border at Carlisle. There were six warehouses and 150 shops in my area. I would have a company car and my office was two miles from home in the warehouse at Pilsworth. I would have access to all records of goods in and out of the shops and warehouses with the power to search and arrest any thief. I accepted the job and my only boss was the head of the Transit Security Department.

I went by train to Nottingham where my boss picked me up and we went to Boots head office at Beeston, a few miles out of the city. It was a massive site. I was introduced to the numerous office staff and in the next two working weeks, learned the intricacies of stock records, both in shops and at H.Q. Every item entering or leaving a shop was recorded daily. That first day I took possession of a Ford Escort.

I was in a good hotel near Trent Bridge, but I found bed and breakfast in a hotel a lonely existence. It was summer and I spent every evening wandering along and sitting beside the River Trent. When the fortnight was over I was glad to start the job I was paid to do. The main warehouse in Heywood was in Taylor St. It was one of three medical warehouses in the country where everything in the chemist part of the business was stored and distributed daily to all shops and other distribution warehouses. Together with security guards at Taylor St, was a male and a female security officer. The two officers searched some of the hundreds of staff every day, but their work was involved only with the two warehouses in Heywood. The male officer Richard Flick, had been a traffic constable and the female officer Margaret Bosher, had previously been a store security officer. She was a very smart attractive lady and together with another pleasant girl Hazel Hill; who was the Taylor St receptionist and telephone operator; they have remained great friends to this day.

A new warehouse manager Sam Hadcroft, had arrived in Heywood with his wife Jessie. They were already friends of Leslie and Eileen Hindmarch and also became our friends. After the disappointment of Greater Manchester Police, I was again working with people who knew me and I realised what a pleasant job I had acquired. I had good working conditions, wonderful places to visit and the knowledge that if Nan wanted to, she could travel around my area with me. She often did just that and sometimes we took our boxer dog Shane along too. I could fill several pages with the memories that I have of where we went together in the next eleven years and our travels through Cheshire, Derbyshire, the Upper Severn Valley, North Wales and Anglesey, the coastal towns of Lancashire and Merseyside and the Lake District were delightful, with the added bonus that I was getting paid for it.

It was very difficult in the first few months to acquire the knowledge needed to understand the in-store records but the supervisors in the back of the stores in Rochdale, Sale, St Helens, St Annes, Southport and Cleveleys were extremely good with me and after six months I got the best monthly results in the country until I retired at 65. Within a few weeks I had secured the first of many arrests. Sale notified me that the driver of the daily lorry was believed to be stealing items from the sales counters early in the morning when he went through the shop to deliver the mail bag. The following day I hid in the shop and watched the driver pick up several items which he put in his pocket. I apprehended him but then had to stay with him until he had completed his round of shops. The driver lived near Matthew Moss School in Rochdale so I told him to drive back to his home where he produced other goods which he had stolen. We then went back to the Depot where he was sacked and I handed him over to the police. He was given a fine in court.

One of the Boots arrests during my police service was the biggest they could ever remember. One of my constables received information that sandals sold by Boots stores were being sold in a public house. Enquiries revealed that one of the depot drivers was a customer. I found out from Leslie Hindmarch what route the driver was on, where he lived and what time he was due back at the depot. The constable and I kept observations on his home in Railway St and in the early afternoon he drove the Boots lorry to the front of his house. He didn't have any sandals, but in his cab were two large pictures and other goods which he had stolen from the shop delivery that day. We arrested him and took him to the police station.

One of my retired sergeants Dick Berry was the security officer for the warehouse. He was called in and as the driver confessed, Dick accompanied my staff and so twelve Boots employees including five drivers were arrested and their homes searched. The police station was full of prisoners and goods. Les Hindmarch came over to value the property, but eventually said, "Please don't arrest any more drivers, I haven't got any more substitutes for tomorrows medical deliveries to our stores." All those arrested pleaded guilty and were dismissed from Boots.

Holidays in Switzerland

1946

This was our very first holiday to Switzerland and the first time that Nan would see her family after seven years in England. We bought our tickets from London to Lucerne from Altham's in Clitheroe for the princely sum of £13 each. Coach tickets from Preston to London were bought from the Ribble bus office at 15s each, all return of course. Our trip was to be for five weeks and we were loaded up with two luggage cases, a carrycot, as our eldest son Ray was just a baby, a knapsack and Nan's shoulder bag. The knapsack held two flasks of hot water, cans of dried baby milk and sandwiches for two days, so off we set. In those days there were no disposable nappies or plastic bags but we did the best we could.

Nan always described this journey the best, so I will try and replicate what she would have said. It was a tale often told to her Inner Wheel colleagues.

So, one afternoon, off we set from Mitchell Street to Bawdlands bus stop which was about 400 yards, then on the Ribble country bus via Hurst Green and Longridge to Preston bus station. The conductor assisted us on and off and helped us to the coach station where we had a couple of hours to wait. Fortunately, the coach wasn't full so we were able to use a couple of spare seats for the carry cot. There were no motorways so we had to travel on the A roads and stopped three times for toilets and refreshments in bus depots at Newcastle under Lyne, Birmingham and Dunstable. We had no sleep, but the baby slept other than for feeds and a change of nappy. At Dunstable we refilled the flasks. At Victoria, the driver again looked after us and suggested a taxi to the railway station which was half a mile away. We couldn't afford one so we walked.

At the railway station, there was a three hour wait so we sat on our suitcases and watched the world go by smiling at the onlookers who gazed at a happy chappie in the carry cot. Once aboard the boat train, it was time once more for a nappy change, then at Dover we went through the customs and onto the British Rail ferry. Railway porters helped passengers with luggage for a 2/ 6d tip.

It was quite a rough crossing to Calais, so Nan spent most of the time outside on the deck to avoid sea-sickness. We didn't need food, but the restaurant filled up our hot water flasks. At Calais, the train was waiting on the dockside and a sailor transferred our luggage. Once again a 2/6d tip was needed. The train was spotlessly clean and although we were in second class, I can remember white linen covers over the seat backs. We never saw any other English people on that train. Every town and village in Northern France had been bombed and shelled. The railways had been shelled so often that frequently it was a single track. On many occasions the engine would detach in a station, then transfer to the rear and pull it back out to re-join the main line.

At each station, French people were getting on and off along with their live animals which had been bought at the markets. Pigs, goats and hens filled the compartments and corridors. They were crowded, but imagine what the toilets were like after two hundred miles… and we still weren't even half way! By evening, the crush diminished and by the time dawn broke we were getting closer to our final destination – Switzerland. The scenery improved no end and although we were desperately tired, the little lad was as good as gold. The kit bag was now full of smelly nappies and empty flasks.

There were very few passengers left as we rolled into Basle and reached the Swiss side of the station. It was marvellous… a different world altogether. I made a 'bee-line' for the men's toilet. Picture the scene… I was standing at the urinal and once I had completed my business, I turned to button up my trousers when I saw a female toilet attendant standing there holding out her hand. Imagine my surprise and shock! When I got back to Nan, she told me that in the railway station it cost 20 Rappen (2p) to have a pee! I didn't go back.

The station restaurant was next on the agenda and we had a continental breakfast. It was the best tasting breakfast of its kind that I had ever had. Then I had a wash and a shave and we joined the train to Lucerne. Nan had brought a little bit of Swiss money with her when she had first arrived in England and she had brought it with her on this trip. The currency had not changed, so she bought our breakfast. Again, and all throughout our holiday we were surrounded by people looking at the baby in his basket. In the ladies room at Basle station, Nan had been able to wash the nappies and so although they were wet, there was no smell.

In Nan's talks to the Inner Wheel, she would have been able to talk about the emotion she must have felt at returning to her home country. I was just as impressed by the scenery... the mountains and lakes all untouched by war. Whilst we had travelled through France, Nan had been speaking in French, but once in Switzerland, she reverted to German which must have been quite a challenge as she was constantly interpreting for my benefit.

The one hour train from Basle to Lucerne passed quickly. As we left the ticket barrier in the majestic Lucerne station, I looked up at the beautiful thirty yard mural of the Rhine Falls, and then outside saw the beautiful city of Lucerne where Nan was born. We knew the Eckerts address, where Nan's sister Gretle lived, but had no idea where it was, so with the remainder of the Swiss money we got a taxi which dropped us off at 22 Mozartstrasse, a detached house on the bank of the Rot See (Red Sea). The rear garden sloped down to the path alongside the lake, which was, and still is, an international rowing venue. The other side of the lake was farmland, full of sheep. It was ecstasy. Even though I had been to Bermuda which some have called paradise, I thought that Switzerland was the most beautiful.

Gretle was Nan's eldest sister and was married to George Eckert, originally German, but now Swiss. They had two children, both similarly named George and Gretle. In those days, George was a millionaire. He renovated paintings and did gilt work with gold leaf. His studio was on the banks of the River Reisse, as it flowed out of the lake. This work was primarily with large churches, hotels, monasteries and even the Vatican. Unfortunately, he was very careful with the money side, but thankfully, Gretle made up for it. He did however buy me a second hand folding camera which I used for the next ten years.

In those five days, Gretle looked after Ray, and George and the children took us round all the places of interest in Lucerne. One morning, we watched the Black Watch pipe band playing their marching tunes on the quay side. The wooden bridge across the river was a wonderful attraction as were the steamers on the lake. Whilst in Lucerne, we walked or cycled everywhere. George took us to see the stage show which told the story of William Tell. We climbed up the seven towers surrounding the city and saw all the wonderful shops in the old part. The day arrived for us to go to Stans and the Eckerts took us on the tram to the lakeside where we boarded the steamer, criss-crossing the lake and getting off at the fifth stop which was Stanstaad. In those days there was no through railway line from Lucerne to Stans. We got on the little red diesel train which only had two carriages and up the valley for two miles to Stans.

I would never be able to recount the joy of that meeting between Nan and her mother, so I am not going to try, but the whole family were on the station platform to greet us. Lots of fuss was made of the baby, and I immediately felt a tremendous liking for Nan's sister Paulette which lasted until the day she died. Nan's mother was a nice petite lady even smaller than Nan.

Before Nan left for England in 1939, the family had lived in a large detached house, so she must have got a surprise when we reached 22 Schmiedgasse and saw the house her family now owned. When her father died and only her mother was living there, their original house was sold and she moved into the house at Schmiedgasse. It had been decided that the house should be Nan's, but Nan wouldn't accept it, saying that her mother and sister Claire should remain in it, but that when eventually her mother died, the house should be sold and the proceeds be shared out between the sisters. It was one of the oldest houses in Stans and her mother and her sister Claire lived on the first floor.

The ground floor and cellar housed a dairy farm shop which was owned by the Barmetli family. Schmiedgasse was quite a narrow street and opposite the dairy were fifty or so stone steps which accessed the next street up the mountainside. Every morning very early, the farmers wearing their clogs clattered down to the dairy to deposit the milk churns which they had carried down the mountainside, and that, together with the church clock chiming every fifteen minutes took a little getting used to.

In the other house, there had been the four sisters: Gretle, Paulette and Claire who were twins and Nan; one adopted sister and a brother. When their father had died, Gretle and George had moved to Lucerne and Seppi, Nan's brother had also died. Paulette and her husband Karl bought the large new house in Bristenstrasse; Claire married, but her husband had also died. The adopted daughter moved to Zurich, married and had a son and a daughter called Trixy. We saw Trixy whilst we were on holiday a few times and I know that Nan never liked her mother. Trixy was the younger child but was a nice girl, probably about 13 or 14 years old.

During that first holiday I met almost everyone who Nan had known before the war, and in particular the Bachmann's – Josie and all the family. Josie Hildebrand was Nan's second cousin and had married Hans Bachmann. Unlike Nan who was a mountaineer and skier, Josie liked cycling and boyfriends, but they got on great together. Josie had three daughters, Lesolette, Ursula and

Hildegarde. The youngest was the same age as Ray. The Hildebrands also lived in Schmiedgasse and went on family picnics up into the mountains then back on a cable car. If we were in Switzerland, we went with them. Hans Bachmann had his own business as a car mechanic, but Lotte his eldest daughter married Weasel, a brilliant radio technician and they built a new workshop and radio technology factory in Stans. Police rescue helicopters would land outside for repairs. Weasel was also a pilot and he flew me in a four-seater plane over the mountains, but once was enough!

Josie was very fond of going to Einsedeln, the beautiful Catholic Cathedral near Switze, the 'Lourdes' of Switzerland. Pilgrims from all over the world would visit to see the Black Madonna. We went with her once on an annual visit and had lunch in a beautiful restaurant. She and Claire would spend a lot of money on a speciality biscuit which Nan also enjoyed. Being in business, the firm used to get free tickets on ski lifts and cable cars, which she used to give to us as cable car rides were always costly. I think they had shares in several mountain railways. One of my photo albums shows some of the places we visited on that holiday as do the postcards. Josie's brother was also called Hans and he took us several times up and over the mountain passes.

During the war, Nan used to speak about the Park and Palace Hotels on Bergenstock, where the very rich people stayed, and on that first holiday, Nan and I walked the seven miles through the forest up to the hotels, 1,400 feet up and overlooking Lake Lucerne. We walked along the narrow path alongside the rock face as far as the 300metre high lift. It would be another two years before we actually went up in the lift. It took us all day as we walked very slowly. Perhaps we should have waited until later years as it was only four months since Nan had given birth to our first child.

We also walked to Stansstad and round the lake to Keyrseten with Ray in the borrowed pram and all of the family. We dined in some lovely lakeside hotels as the Swiss didn't believe in cooking on a Sunday. Another delight was hiring a rowing boat at Stansstad or Furigen and rowing four miles across the lake to a hotel on the lakeside at Kastaniabaum, where we had an ice-cream and then we would row back.

Stanserhorn, in the early years was negotiated by three separate cable track railways with two midway stations. Claire and Nan's mother took us up to the first station and we walked back down alongside the track picking blackberries. On Sunday's the Swiss all went to church, mainly Roman Catholic, and an enormous number would be dressed in their national costumes. It was lovely to see, plus the sound of yodelling and Alpine Horns. Each village had a brass band, flag throwers and a yodel choir and there were processions galore.

In this first holiday we stayed mainly in the area near Stans but all the places we visited had post cards, and I started to collect them from each place we visited. The family often bought me a card to put in an old album which they also gave me and throughout the years I continued to collect a card at each venue. Nan never spoke about her brother having had a girlfriend, but his best friend Max came to see her several times. He had taken her brother's place as head of the County's Physical Training Instructors. He was married to a blonde bombshell and they also lived in Schmiedgasse. What sort of emotions must Nan have felt? She could have been talking to her lovely brother Seppi, if he had not been killed whilst piloting a Swiss Air Force plane during the war.

I met Nan's favourite school friend Elsie Yoller, who was the daughter of the mayor of Stans. She became engaged then married a major in the Swiss army. As they moved away, we only ever saw her once again, when we visited them on a later holiday. We often borrowed bicycles and used to cycle to Lucerne around the lakeside. There was little traffic in those days.

Claire was a dressmaker and was associated to a local bazar which kept her occupied. Paulette, Nan's favourite sister and mine, was married to Karl and they had a ski wax and paint business. Karl was the president of the local ski club. When Karl went off to the different places of business he took us with him to Zurich, Bern and other places. Just before our visit, he had an accident with his car and got done for drunk-driving. He was given a fine and banned from driving for three months but asked the police if the ban could start after we returned to England and they granted his request.

Switzerland had been isolated and neutral throughout the war and it was full of Italian families who the Swiss had employed as labourers, and it was these men who had built the new Susten Pass road. Eventually the Swiss repatriated them all back to Italy.

During the third week, I received notification that I had passed the Police exam, but asked if I would join Liverpool City Police as they were very understaffed. I agreed and gave them the date of my return. An appointment was awaiting me when we returned from holiday.

That first holiday in Switzerland was so wonderful. It had been a magnificent five weeks, never to be forgotten, but the time came for us to leave for Basle in Karl's car with far more luggage than we had arrived, presents and loads of chocolates plus a heavier baby in the carry cot. I feel that I can remember every minute of it, and it was a tearful parting to return home, but we knew we would be able to return on holiday every two years and when we got our own car in 1958, we made this an annual visit. Claire had opened a Swiss bank account for Nan which she contributed to monthly. We were far better off leaving Switzerland than we had been on the outward trip.

Back home I joined the Liverpool City Police as Constable 187E, at Walton. Nan never needed to be employed and was happy as the wife of a policeman, saving up for whatever we required.

1948

To leave England I had to get permission from the Superintendent at Accrington. In 1948 we returned for our next two week holiday to Stans. It was the same journey as before, but we had no carrycot or nappies this time as Ray was now two years old. We took the bus to Preston, then the overnight bus to London. We had a little longer to wait in London for the train, so we spent three hours with friends of mine from Clitheroe who lived in Epping on the edge of the forest. Pat and Sid Marfleet had four sons. We deposited our luggage in the left luggage department at the station and went to Epping on the tube. Having a meal with them did help to break the journey.

It was the same set up at Dover where we had the help of porters on and off the ferry, but at Calais we found that our train was going to Paris. There were no animals this time but we had to change stations in Paris which was a short journey accompanied by a porter, who wanted additional money but he didn't get it. It was still an overnight journey to Basel, then a train to Lucerne, and the steamer to Stansstad and then we boarded the little red train to Stans. I nick-named this train, 'The Stanser Express.' There were not as many people there to meet us but the welcome was nevertheless very warm, and thankfully we weren't quite as tired as on our previous trip.

For the first time we went to Engelberg which was the terminus for the Stanser Express and then we went on the fifteen miles up a very steep gradient to the famous ski resort. We then went on a steep track mountain railway and then a large cable car over a tremendous valley up to the ice and snow of Trubsee. A single seat then took us further up. This was one of the places where Nan, as a girl accompanied her brother on his mountain climbs up to the summit of Titlis. Later, I was able to go further by cable car over the glaciers to the top of Titlis; a wonderful journey. There were thirty four cable cars and ski lifts in the valley between Stans and Engelberg. We visited Engelberg twice in those two weeks. The second visit was to go up a cable car on a different valley to view the Titlis mountain range.

We again rode bikes to Lucerne, but this time Ray was sitting behind me. We were still reliant on the family who were taking us further and further afield, but it wasn't until I had my own car in 1958 that we really did go to town travelling throughout Switzerland and into Austria, Germany and Italy.

1950's

In *1950* Clive was born so that year we went to Switzerland with two boys. 1950 was the year I saw the Rhone Glacier for the first time. This is the beginning of the River Rhone which ends in the Mediterranean Sea. The glacier was almost down to the valley bottom and we were able to go inside along a boardwalk. It was a beautiful blue colour. When I last went to see it in 2005, the glacier had almost disappeared.

In *1952* we again travelled by coach and train and Ray was now six years old and Clive two. I had always wanted to climb up Stanserhorn using the footpath which for most of the way bordered the railway except of course it zig-zagged. At four am one morning, long before sunrise I set off with Ray and we finally reached the top at eight thirty. The middle section which was very close to the railway was through a forest and very steep. At each upward turn, Ray, who was walking in front said, "Oh heck!"

The top section as we left the second station gave us a view of tremendous scenery. In the midst the beautiful mountain flowers which Stanserhorn was famous for, we were walking with the mountain goats which attached themselves to us. It was an exhausting, but exhilarating climb and we took this last section easy. The sun was shining, but it was a relief when we reached the level top and went into the very old stone built Stanserhorn Hotel.

We took our boots off and went in for a breakfast, six thousand feet up, the first visitors of the day.

The railway station was in the lower part of the building. There were twenty apartments overlooking Stans with three separate storeys, but on the opposite side it was a single storey, being the front of the hotel. The ground fell away steeply into a valley used by Stans Ski Club. The outlook was that of the entire Bernese Oberland Mountains which included The Eiger, Monch and Jungfrau. The hotel was closed during the winter months as was the mountain railway. Apparently a Swiss couple looked after the hotel during the winter, but a few years later the hotel burned down completely and a wooden building replaced it, but it was never the same. Ray and I returned via the railway. Many years later, Nan and I walked up and then descended via the other side to Dalenweil. That was some journey and we were shattered, but happy.

In *1954* we thought it would be nice for Nan to take the boys a week before I got my two weeks holiday, then I would go on my own with most of the luggage and join them. Off they went with a request that Nan would send me a telegram when she arrived. I got the telegram two days later which said, 'Arrived safe. Clive fell off the train.' It was only when I arrived in Switzerland that I found out exactly what had happened. Having managed on the two buses and train to Dover, the boys were very tired and as they alighted from the train at Dover, Nan held each boy by the hand. However, Clive's hand slipped from her grasp and he disappeared between the running board of the train and the platform edge. The other passengers, as well as Nan, were horrified, but two little hands appeared and he was picked from the narrow gap unhurt.

That week on my own I was on night duty, so after refreshments I would pick up our dog 'Tache' and take him round Clitheroe until 5am when I dropped him at home. Nan did enjoy her extra week, but I must admit that it never happened again; we always went together thereafter.

This was the year when we went later in the year and the cows were brought down from the mountains, to the lower pastures. Hundreds would walk through the village, bedecked with garlands of flowers and the cow bells ringing. This was also the year when Nan told me about the skulls in the crypt of Stans Church. We went down to have a look at them and there were hundreds on ledges. Stans cemetery is a lovely serene place which has a little chapel and it is in this little chapel that the 'Lussi' family crest takes its place amongst fifteen other family crests on the window. Bodies are only left in the ground for fifty years and then their families, if so desired, could have the skulls placed in the church crypt until such time as it was full. When I saw it, it was already full, so what happens to the bodies now I have no idea, but they are still removed after fifty years.

We often went to the Lido at Stanstaad with the two boys, but we found a more beautiful spot with a free car park by the side of Lake Lucerne at Buochs. It became our picnic spot, but like many other places in Switzerland, it eventually became spoiled by a motorway which was built close by and so parking became restricted. Motorways can be very useful, but not in a very beautiful country like Switzerland. It was always so nice to wander along the narrow mountain roads. The motorway toll for a year was thirty francs which I think has now risen to forty.

On this holiday we took one of our longest walks ever in Switzerland. We went to Buochs on a bus and then went with Claire and the boys on a cable car to Furigen, just a hamlet on the mountainside above Buochs, then we started walking across the mountains, round the back of Buochserhorn and with Brisen on the left we eventually reached Dallenwil. It was a very hot sunny day. The sun was always on our left and when we reached Dallenwil, Nan who was wearing a short sleeved blouse realised that she had been sunburned. Fortunately, we were able to get some quick attention, and apart from having to avoid the sun for a few days, she quickly recovered, but it taught us a lesson.

Lynne was born in 1955 so in *1956* we went to Switzerland by air. We went on the express bus to Manchester, now with three children and we flew by Swiss Air to Zurich. Karl was waiting for us. It certainly was our first trip in style and we returned the same way, with extra weight in our cases but in those days there were no restrictions on baggage.

In January *1958*, Nan's mother Briggita had died whilst we were in Clitheroe and sadly Nan had not been able to get to her funeral. 1958 was the year we had moved to Rawtenstall and our next door neighbours were P.C. Frank Fairclough and his wife Phyllis who had no children.

Frank had been a traffic policeman and was accustomed to driving large vehicles so we asked them if they would like to come with us and decided that we would hire a small minivan in Switzerland. They were delighted to accept so again we travelled from Manchester to Zurich by Swiss Air and we took possession of a minivan at the airport for two weeks.

Frank and I shared the driving and although it wasn't the newest of vehicles, with his knowledge, we kept it going. We travelled all over Switzerland, even down to the Italian border at Lugano and Locarno. We stayed on a camp site and the weather was lovely and warm. At four am the children were in the swimming pool. Claire, now living alone enjoyed their company and travelled with us quite often. Phyllis was a very cheerful girl and all the family liked her. The holiday was a success, but I had the feeling that Frank was glad to see the back of the minibus.

In *1960* I bought my first car, a second hand Simca. I joined the 'AA' and I still have the badge. I obtained route directions from the 'AA', changed the headlight beams from left to right and off we set. There were no motorways and we had lunch at Lichfield opposite the cathedral, then through London to Dover. We had an overnight stop at a 'bed and breakfast' and parked the car outside. Our luggage was strapped to the roof-rack covered by a tarpaulin. We were in the front bedroom, but I didn't sleep a wink worrying about the luggage. It was because of the necessity to leave the luggage on the roof, that on the next trip we made to Switzerland we decided to find a camp site in France and so In between Arras and Reims we found one at La Fere. It was the local football field and we were the only ones on it, so it was a peaceful overnight stop and I got a good rest.

After breakfast we queued up to board the British ferry to Calais and the challenge of right hand side driving. On the same ship was my Art teacher from Ribblesdale School who was towing a caravan on his first trip abroad. He seemed quite nervous of the challenge of driving on the right hand side of the road and so as I was going towards Paris and that was his destination, I suggested that he follow me as far as Arras. We stopped just before Arras and he brewed up in his caravan before we parted. I have never seen him since.

At Arras which was seventy miles from the coast, we took the route through the First World War battle fields to Reims; a further one hundred and twenty miles. Every village in Flanders had a War Cemetery, all well-known names and we stopped at several. It was interesting, but very sad to see the hundreds and hundreds of well-tended graves as we thought back to that terrible war. Millions of red poppies grew beside the roads and in the fields. That first road journey has left an indelible image in my mind. French farmers and their families were tending the fields with very few tractors and in one parking spot that we chose, on a hilltop overlooking a deep valley we could see the valley on the other side which we would descend. It was almost like a scene from the Bible. An old peasant lady with two sheep dogs came into sight with a flock of about thirty sheep and as the sheep grazed, she sat amongst them. We left after about an hour and she was still sitting there. Throughout all the years we travelled by road, we always stopped in the same place, but we never saw the shepherdess with her sheep again.

The places we travelled through are etched on my memory: Vitry, Chalons sur Marne, Langres, and Belfort. It was four hundred and twenty miles from Calais to the Swiss border at Basel. One of our favourite resting spots was ten miles from the Swiss border and we could see all the Swiss mountains in the distance.

As a point of interest, we never saw any toilets on the journey, it was a case of disappearing from sight and trust to luck that you weren't seen. Many years later, the Mayor and Mayoress of Heywood had a holiday with us in Switzerland and en-route through France on our return journey, the ladies were desperate and had to go behind a hedge. We hadn't realised that the train line was over the other side of the hedge and an express train thundered past. Apparently, Elsie had her bottom towards the track so what sort of view the passengers got has only to be imagined.

The custom office at Basel wouldn't see many G.B. cars in those early years and then it was easy to follow the Lucerne road signs as we passed through the city centre. It was seventy miles to Lucerne, but the route took us over a high pass in the mountains. Later a new motorway was created through the mountain. The Swiss were without motorways until much later so passes were quite perilous in those early times. However, very tired, we would arrive in Lucerne with another ten miles to go round the lakeside bringing us to Stans and a much needed rest.

There was space for our car outside Schmiedgasse. A grapevine hung alongside the front door and opposite was the beer garden of a small inn, 'Three Kings' and next to that was an old people's home. The Mayor's home was forty yards away and this was a gent's outfitters. Claire had continued with her dress making but it was an emotional time for Nan, not to have her mother waiting for us. We missed her, but it did create an extra room. Claire had made our arrival her holiday time and if we weren't going too far, we fitted her in and Lynne, now three, sat on Nan's knees. Claire did all the cooking, but on Sundays everybody in Switzerland seemed to go out for Sunday lunch. Transport always arrived and we would go about twenty miles to a lovely hotel in the mountains beyond Kerns. It was always the same waitress and I often wondered if she recognised us on our bi-annual visits.

Stans is the main town of the Canton of Nidwalden and between it and Engelberg lie thirty four cable cars and ski lifts. Engelberg is a well-known ski centre. In the centre of Stans was the Dorfplatz, the village square which contained the church. Alongside this was a marble monument of Arnold Von Winkelried, a Swiss soldier who in the Austrian-Swiss war, bravely threw himself onto a row of the pikes of the Hapsburg army which enabled his comrades to advance and so led the Swiss to victory. Nan said that the children's version of this story was that he was pushed!

Stans was the annual venue of a large procession, when all the Swiss Counties sent a group and they processed round the town. It took two hours to pass and included horses, cattle, tractors, carts, musicians, bell ringers, flag throwers, horn blowers, bands, and yodellers all in the different Canton National costumes, and it finished up in the College playing field. It was a wonderful sight!

Another special feature of the town was that they supported a charity for poor children. Each year, Switzerland struck a set of stamps called 'Pro Juventute', and each stamp had an excess charge of ten cents. The ten cents were given to the Pro Juventute Charity. Every year, for one day, Schmeidgasse was blocked off to vehicles and every resident had a garden party; a joyous town booze-up, was my interpretation of it; but it really was good fun with lots of food and beer and a party which never became violent even though it lasted well into the night. The resultant large sum of money was sent to the Pro Juventute Foundation. There was always something going on, Cumberland style wrestling, a tug of war, shooting and hang gliding.

I found the Swiss people very affable until one day

when I was with Nan and Paulette in my car and I was waiting to turn out of a side road into the main street, when an elderly (80 ish!) lady driving a posh car turned into the side street, clobbered my front wing and carried on until I saw her stop at a large house. Paulette knew her and asked her why she didn't stop. Her reply was, "he backed into me!" Two local bobbies came out at our request and they told us that they had been trying to stop her from driving for several years. They were pleased because this was their chance to ban her immediately. I was told to call in at a local garage the following morning at 7am and my car would be repaired at her expense... and it was.

The journey back from this holiday could have been a disaster, but we survived. After leaving Switzerland, one of my wheels went into a pothole and it broke one of my rear springs and I lost first and second gear. It was morning and I stopped at two garages to see if they could assist. I had a French car, but they weren't interested! Nan was concerned and said, "What are we going to do?" We had automobile insurance but I decided to get into third gear and see if we could reach Calais, three hundred and twenty miles away. The three children in the back weren't a bit concerned. Never travelling faster than thirty miles an hour, and even with two large diversions, we arrived ten hours later at the docks in Calais and immediately boarded the ferry.

Whilst on the ship, a man came to me and said, "Have you driven a Simca today?" I told him I had and he informed me that he had passed us twice that day, having stopped for meals. At Dover, I then started the long night time journey back to Rossendale. Seville's bakery repaired my car the following day. That near disaster which caused me to travel quite slowly, made me consider the possibility of driving through France at night and increasing my speed up to fifty miles an hour! From that year on, I drove the eight hundred and twenty mile journey in just twenty four hours. If I felt tired I pulled into a lay-by or service area and slept for whatever time I needed. Nan and the children had blankets and slept through the night undisturbed. I don't recommend this to others, but I didn't have any problems.

In later years when we living in Heywood, I replaced the Simca with a new Morris Oxford; a much heavier and roomier vehicle. It was a solid machine and I liked it. Ray was eighteen and decided that he wanted to stay behind. Unfortunately, when he left for work one morning, the kitchen window was left open and a burglar entered. It was obviously a youth, as all that was taken was my entire collection of football and cricket cups. He actually left the largest cup at the front door because he picked up Nan's new sewing machine instead of the trophy. We never found out who the culprit was as none of the items were ever traced.

As the years rolled by, our three children were married and Nan and I went on holiday on our own, occasionally travelling through Belgium and Germany for a change and even on one occasion going through Luxembourg. In those years, we were able to travel throughout the whole of the country, up most of the mountains and even into Bavaria, Lichtenstein, Austria and Italy. We took Paulette and Claire with us and they said that they saw more of their country with us than they ever had before. We were able to stay away overnight and once found ourselves lost in the Italian Dolomite Mountains in Italy.

Occasionally, friends would accompany us in separate cars and we used to hire a chalet which was a third of the way up Stanserhorn and from the chalet was a beautiful view overlooking the town. It had been owned by one of the Stanserhorn train drivers. Doreen and Stanley Jackson stayed at the chalet with us, but unfortunately, Doreen snored so loudly that Nan couldn't sleep, even though there were two rooms between us. She made an excuse after the first night to sleep in the town at Paulette's, so that she could pick up fresh bread rolls for breakfast and I would collect her. It was the loudest snoring I've ever heard.

Occasionally, our children with their families would also have a holiday with us in Stans and used the chalet. Clive and Anne and the girls, Andrea and Lyndsey were in the South of France when the very hot weather caused forest fires near the campsite where they were staying, so they came up to Switzerland. Anne and Clive stayed in the Three Kings Gasthaus, whilst the girls stayed with us. That year, the French fishermen went on strike on the Channel coast. The news came that the Channel ports would be closed within forty eight hours, so Clive immediately set off for Calais. They were able to catch the last ferry before the port was blocked off by fishing boats. We had to overstay our holiday by a few days before the blockage ceased and we were able to return. Calais was blocked again on another year, but we diverted to Zeebrugge in Belgium and returned home via Felixstowe.

During our journeys through France we always carried sufficient food and drinks to reach our destination. Nan always made bacon and egg pie and together with French bread and the odd lay-bys where French fries were available, we were never short.

Whilst together, we would often go up small mountains by cable cars and then if possible walk it down by the available paths back to our car. I must say that Stanserhorn was our favourite. On two occasions we walked up one side and down the other to Dallenwil.

Nan and I left Stans one year knowing that Claire was unwell with breast cancer. It was a sad 'goodbye', but she did survive until the following year. She was in and out of Stans hospital, but was home to greet us. We knew that she hadn't long to live and within a few days she had to return to hospital. Paulette and Nan visited her but she became too ill to know who was with her. Paulette, Robbie and Reine decided that rather than wait at home for her to die; we would go up to the forest on the Brunig Pass and go to a meadow full of mountain flowers to a spot which Claire loved. It was an emotional afternoon looking across the valley to the Susten and Grimsel Passes, thinking of Claire dying.

When we returned, a very nice gentle lady had passed away. We slept in Scheimidgasse that night. Of course, the house was Nan's but many years before, she had said that if anything happened to Claire, she would split the money from the sale of the house with the Eckert and Frick families.

We decided that I would go back home the following day and Nan would stay at Paulette's until the funeral, then fly back to Manchester. Claire had a beautiful, valuable fur coat which Paulette gave to Nan, together with a full solid silver cutlery set. Had Nan not come to England in 1939, she too would have received a cutlery set, so Paulette thought it only right that Nan have Claire's set. I put them in the boot of my car together with the luggage and left the house for the final time, knowing I had that eight hundred and twenty mile journey to do alone.

It was alright until I reached the large city of Rheims. I entered it on the correct dual carriageway, but many miles away, as I was exiting, I realised that I was on my way to Paris, not St Quentin. With no word of French, and everyone I stopped not a word of English, I somehow found a way back half way to the city centre where I found the correct road to St Quentin, thence to Arras and Calais.

All I wanted to do was to get home. I had completely forgotten about the expensive stuff that I had in the boot, and even when I reached Dover and produced my passport to the lady customs officer, I never gave it a thought.

I just said, "I am alone. My wife's sister has died and my wife is flying back." She waved me straight through and it was only when I reached home and got my luggage, did I realise I could have been locked up for not declaring the goods in my car.

Claire's funeral was a week later and Nan found that last week very distressing. She helped Paulette to dispose of different items in the house and arranged for the house to be sold to Barmetli who owned the dairy next door. The front of the house had to be kept as before, but the rest was annexed to the neighbouring house and fully converted into a luxurious large house with a balcony still overlooking the Three Kings beer garden and the front garden of the Old Folks' Home. Nan's portion of the money was banked and it gave us an annual holiday until after she herself died in 1991. The money in fact lasted until 2005.

After Claire's death, Paulette converted the top storey of her house at 14 Brissenstrasse into a penthouse with instructions that it should be available to the Wilson family as long as necessary. It had previously been a store room and a drying room for the washing. The only fault with it was that it became quite hot in mid-summer and it was necessary to use a cool air fan. Opening windows invited mosquitos. There was a paddling pool in the front garden but it was only two feet deep. Most evenings it was warm and we would either sit on the balcony or in the garden drinking wine whilst watching the sun set over Mount Pilatus. There was always the sound of cow bells from Stanserhorn and even the town meadows. Alpine horns and yodellers were also a familiar sound, but it was a peaceful environment. Even though we knew we would be back in the next year or two, it was always sad to part.

Nan's favourite sister was Paulette and I could understand why. She was very smart and generous with a lovely personality. When she died a few years after Claire, it was never quite the same. Nan flew over for her funeral and when she returned, she said, "Everyone will miss her!" How right she was.

Paulette's house was shared between her three daughters, but Reina paid Elsie and Gretli out and now owns the large house. Many years ago it was valued at one million pounds. Reina had married Robert Holzer, an Austrian who came to Stans as a hairdresser, but eventually was able to buy the gents and ladies salon in Stans. He died in his late sixties due to skin cancer. Robbie always enjoyed lying in the sun. He was a nice man and he and Reina had two daughters Sylvia and Esther who are both married; each with two children. Sylvia and her family live in the ground floor flat and Reina has the first floor. The second floor is rented out.

Karl and Paulette's house was built during the war and he knew that the field in front would never be built on. The ground floor had been his office and storerooms, and the cellar together with a large single storey building at the rear, were his workshops. He made ski wax and paint.

The Retirement Years

Farewell to Switzerland

In 1990, whilst in Switzerland, Nan and I had gone into the Lauterbrunnen Valley, one of our favourite places. We were going to go up on a cable car when Nan chose to sit on a river bank. I should have realised that something was wrong, but Nan had reason to believe that she had cancer. She didn't tell me until the end of the holiday when we reached home and she was seen by her doctor Mrs Williams who was a friend of hers in the Inner Wheel Club. Very quickly, she was sent into Bury Hospital and her left breast was removed. The wound in her breast soon healed, but an incision in her upper left arm never healed and her arm was always swollen and she lost the use of it. Chemotherapy and radiotherapy at Christie's hospital didn't work, but she wouldn't let it stop her from doing what she always did, particularly attending St Luke's Church every Sunday morning and taking Holy Communion.

In early October 1991, we went on a holiday to South Wales with Doreen and Stanley Jackson and Matt and Anne Ingoe, to a farmhouse in Pembrokeshire. It was a nice holiday, but two days before the end, Nan became ill and I brought her home. Dr Williams said that she was anaemic and an ambulance came and took us to Bury General Hospital. Awaiting the arrival of the ambulance, she sat on a chair in our front doorway looking out at Knowle Hill and our lovely front garden. It was as though she knew she would not see it again.

I stayed with her until a bed was found and I returned home thinking she would be alright. The following morning, on the sixteenth of October, I bought her a new nightie from M&S and went to see her with a large bunch of flowers for the two pm visiting hour. I was told that doctors were attending to her as she was seriously ill with blood poisoning and wouldn't survive.

The doctors departed and I was allowed to visit her in the ward. She was on oxygen and very ill but she knew I was there. Our three children arrived as well as the Rev, Clifford Knowles. She was moved into a side ward and we all stayed with her. At ten pm, as we said The Lord's Prayer, she passed peacefully away from earth to heaven. Her remembrance service was at St Luke's, the church she loved. Over two hundred people attended and the Townswomen's Guild Choir sang the twenty third Psalm, The Lord is my Shepherd. Reina and Gretli came from Switzerland.

This was the eulogy which the vicar read out at Nan's funeral service on the 23rd October 1991.

Nan Wilson R.I.P.

'Last Sunday evening there was a programme on television in which one of the principal characters said there's a vast difference between a photograph and a portrait of a person. Unlike the photograph which reproduces the finest detail, a portrait reveals a person's inner character, their true self in fact.

If I were to ask you for your portrait of Nan, no doubt all would be different and yet all contain something of the truth of a lovely lady, and a lady in the real sense, whose life we celebrate and whose death we mourn today. Nobody can say everything there is to say about another human being. My task therefore is to try, albeit humbly and inadequately, to present a portrait of Nan from what I knew of her and about her, and to trust that in so doing it will add a bit more to the picture which God alone can and will complete.

Born in Switzerland near Lucerne, Nan came to England to learn the language shortly before the outbreak of World War Two. She lived and worked in Clitheroe for a family of wealthy mill owners, from whom she partly acquired her high standards for good food and housekeeping. Her duties took her to the G.P.O. as it then was, and there she met Jack. I don't know who swept the other off their feet but suffice to say they were married in 1943 at Gospel Hall. A true partnership for 48 years, Nan longed for it to reach 50 but sadly that was not to be. She was however blessed with a lovely family in Ray, Clive and Lynne and their respective partners Barbara, Anne and John, 6 grandchildren and two nieces in Switzerland; Gretle and Reina, and it's good that they are able to be here today for this service. It's to Jack and the family especially, that our hearts go out today and I would assure them of our love, our prayers and our support at this particularly sad time.

Although family life was the centre of Nan's world she had other interests and achievements too. She mastered for example 5 languages, English, German, French, Italian and Swiss dialect, and when Heywood became twinned with Peine, Nan was the official interpreter. She first became involved with the Townswomen's Guild in 1964 and although not a member of the choir was 'adopted' by them and accompanied them on trips abroad. It was appropriate therefore that they should pay their tribute musically to her today. Nan had been connected with the Inner Wheel since 1965 and served as their President twice. The consequence was that she was well known and well loved. Always cheerful, even when in pain, forever courteous and welcoming, the only time I heard her say something derogatory about anybody was fairly recently when she advised me not to accept Jack's offer of a cup of tea, which she said was only marginally better than Hilda's coffee!

Placid and easy-going, always looking for the best in others, ever helpful to all in need, her death will leave a gap in many lives.

In her spare time she read a lot, adored the countryside, the scenery especially, and gained as much pleasure from a bunch of wild flowers as from the most delicate orchids.

Jack says she was good with scissors – that is, cutting the flowers he grew to give away to friends. She had some very dear friends who gave her immense pleasure and the number of condolence cards received by all the family tells how much she was loved and respected.

It was about ten years ago that Nan started coming to St. Luke's and immediately felt at home here. She loved the building and the people and for her part was a most faithful communicant. Even when she was ill, she came to church Sunday by Sunday and set an example in faithfulness to God to inspire us all. Obviously a lady with many good qualities to her life, the one above all for which I will remember was her tremendous courage in the midst of terrible pain. Her spirit was such that she refused to give in, rejected the offer of analgesics and battled on. It was good that her death came in the manner befitting her nature – very gently and peacefully and surrounded by her family.

As we remember Nan today we say thank you to God for the gift of her life, for the very real contribution to God's world and for the fact that all our lives are the richer for having known her.

Death is most certainly not the end for Nan. The last word always belongs to God! He defeated death on Easter Day and this service finds its true meaning in Christ's resurrection. Indeed all our lives find their real meaning and true purpose in God. Sadness is inevitable when a loved one dies but in it and through it, the love and care of God are there. He will neither desert us nor fail us and is never closer than in our moments of greatest need.

Nan's suffering is now ended and she rests in the peace of the God whom she loved and trusted. He will take good care of her and one day you will meet again. So then with love, with thanks and with hope in our hearts, we prepare to commit Nan's earthly body into God's gracious keeping with our prayers.'

Nan's ashes were spread under a beautiful red Hawthorne

203

tree in the Church graveyard at the altar end outside St Luke's Church. Every Sunday, I left a small bunch of flowers where her ashes were and it has left a small hollow in the grass amongst the crocuses and daffodils which I planted. She was greatly loved and having helped to bring up her six grandchildren, she is still loved by them and they often speak about her twenty two years later. After her death, my family were close around me, but it was also nice to be with friends, particularly my closest friends, Hilda and Geoffrey Hanson and Doreen and Stanley Jackson. Doreen had just bought the wool to make a kneeler for the front of the altar at St Luke's. The cost of the materials used to make the kneeler was £260, so I gave her half and asked if I could help and dedicate it in memory of Nan. She agreed and for many, many hours I did the easy stitching and she did the ornate parts. It is still the altar kneeler and still as good as new.

An Inspiring model

At the same time as Nan died, Ronald Booth, a parishioner of All Soul's Church also lost his wife. He came to see me and we chatted for about an hour. I realised that he was just as devastated about the loss of his wife as I was about losing Nan, but unlike my situation where I had a supportive family to help; his two daughters had fallen out with him. I arranged to see him a few days later and it was a much longed for conversation. I was able to meet his daughters who were reconciled with their father and this was the start of our friendship. By the end of our chat, I realised that we had to do something to help us both out of the pain we were in and keep us focussed.

Ron, a retired joiner had previously made a model of All Soul's Church in 1987, but since then he had lost the use of his hands through severe arthritis. I decided that together we could make a model of St Luke's Church. I would pay for it and make the detailed parts under his guidance, using his expertise as a joiner. Photos were taken of the outside of the church and using a floor plan we were able to make the model to scale. Previously unable to make anything out of wood, I worked with Ron for sixteen months building the model church on his kitchen table at his home. We got on well and the whole experience was therapy for us both. Coloured negatives of the stained glass windows were made and used to put into the model as exact copies of the existing windows. It was made in sections that slotted together, the doors opening with tiny hinges. However, the steeple was never taken to the height it should have been or it would not have fitted into Ron's kitchen. The final window was ready to go in, but I was off to Scotland so I left it with Ron to complete. He did, but died just afterwards in his home at the age of 81, alone with his beloved model. I completed the model with the assistance of a friend of Ron, putting lighting in and a tape which plays music from Canterbury Cathedral. When the lights were switched on, organ music played. Sadly, he never lived to see it inside St Luke's Church, where it is today. Visitors who appreciate the work and dedication which went into the model are encouraged to donate to the Church restoration fund.

Working for Others

Throughout my life, I have worked in the service of others; in the Navy and as a policeman. Charity work became a natural part of our lives and Nan and I were both actively working for several charities for many years. In 1965, I was invited to join the Heywood Rotary Club and Nan the Inner Wheel. I was the president of the Rotary in 1973/74 and Nan was president of the Inner Wheel twice; in 1970/71 and 1979/80. We were proud members of this organisation and it was very enjoyable for us both as everybody in the two clubs were friends. There were many parties and get-togethers in the various homes of the members, several being at Jesmond Dene.

I remember one Inner Wheel party when there were

thirty three ladies in my front room. Bonfire Night was always celebrated with a big bonfire and the ever popular black peas and again charity collections were made. These bonfires were held at Links Road until the new houses were built, then the final two years saw one at Heywood Cricket Club and then at the Church Inn where my four youngest grandchildren helped to build and then ignite it.

Coffee mornings, bring and buy sales, and garden parties amongst many other events filled our spare time. We attended church each Sunday; I played sport and we were always very busy people. Nan organised a group of ladies to hold whist drives at their respective homes every fortnight and the money raised was given to charity. As well as being the town's official translator, Nan worked tirelessly for the Inner Wheel and the Townswomen's Guild. She translated for the official town twinning with Peine in Germany and attended many events supporting their work. As a member of St Luke's Church, she also organised the coffee after morning service at the church which continued for many years.

In 1974, when I was the President of the Rotary, Heywood's status as a Borough came to an end and to mark the occasion, a Victorian 'Old Time Music Hall' was held at the Civic Hall organised once again by the Rotary. We dressed authentically, some as old time bar tenders, waitresses and many ladies came in their Victorian costumes. I was dressed in a black beard, red tasselled hat and seaman's sweater with the initials RNLI on it. The Ashton Repertory theatre Company provided the entertainment, giving their time free of charge supplying the audience with a constant stream of jokes, songs, sketches, dancing and comedy.

Fund raising events for charities such as Cancer Research, The Institute for the Blind, the Lifeboat Association, St John's Ambulance, muscular dystrophy and several oversees charities were often organised by the Rotary Club or Inner Wheel. Emergency boxes were often made up by the members of the Rotary and Inner Wheel to provide essentials in case of world disaster and many lorry loads were sent all over the world. Local charities such as those which helped the older folk were never forgotten and at Christmas, collections would be made as members went carol singing and stood for hours on the market with collecting boxes.

In the year that I was Rotary President, I asked Father Duggan of St Joseph's Catholic Church if we could borrow the figures of the 'Holy Family' to parade around the town on the back of a small truck. We would knock on doors asking people if they would like to donate to the Heywood Christmas Charities. After promising to be very careful with the figures, we loaded them onto the truck with a couple of bales of straw fastening the stable securely with rope. As we went up Bury Road, a sudden gust of wind blew the roof of the stable off, landing on the road with the head of Joseph beside it. This was certainly not the Christmas story as it was told in the Bible! The following day, I tried to explain what had happened to Father Duggan, but he seemed unflustered saying, "Don't worry lad!" Joseph was put back together again, given a new coat of paint and was looking as good as new by Christmas Day.

The following year we dared not risk the journey around the town again with the Holy Family, so I asked the market if they would allow us to display it there. In those days, the market was a stone's throw away from the Church and so not as much of a risk to poor Joseph. It was a resounding success! Helping to pack up on the Saturday evening was my grandson Nicholas; then aged fourteen. He passed a shepherd up onto the lorry, but the Rotarian who was in front of him stumbled and Nick had to quickly step out of the way. As the shepherd swung outwards, it knocked the head clean off the donkey. More profuse apologies were given to Father Duggan, who accepted them in his usual gracious manner, and the donkey was repaired for Christmas Day.

Another year passed and thanks to the kindness of

Father Duggan we were once more allowed to borrow the figures with the usual warning to be careful. After yet another successful time collecting for our Christmas Charities, we began to load the figures up onto the lorry again. The Rotarians were reminded to be careful but as one of them lifted the ox up by the horns, they came off in his hands! For the third year running I had to go back to Father Duggan with a tale of woe. He must have had the patience of a Saint! Once again the ox was repaired, but this time there was a bonus... father Duggan contacted me in the New Year to explain that he had been given a legacy with which to buy a new set of crib figures and that he wanted the Rotary to keep the old ones! Used for a few years until the old market shut down, they were then stored in the cellar of the Yorkshire Bank until in 2001, when the Rotary Club offered them to a 'good home'. Where they are now, no-one knows.

One of the biggest fund raising activities which I organised was 'The Great Paper Chase'. Every week, members of the Rotary collected waste paper and card. It was cut, baled and taken to a local waste paper firm to be sold. This was a long term project and members gave their free time each week, working hard to collect the paper from firms and businesses in Heywood using their own transport and labour free of charge. The money raised was destined for a special fund which could be used for any special purpose that might arise. In the event of a disaster in the town, or a chronic case of need arising, the club would then be in a position to offer help quickly.

We were often invited to Mayoral events and afterwards, would be invited to go back to their homes, but two of the Mayors had small houses and so 'Jesmond Dene' became their destination. Each year at the inauguration of the new Mayor, the Liberal Alderman and Councillors with their wives went out for an evening meal and Nan and I were always invited. This was an invitation which we always accepted gracefully.

When Nan died in 1991, we had completed twenty six

years of helping good causes. It had been great doing things together, but going to functions alone was alien to me and I resigned from the Rotary Club. In recognition of my service, I was presented with a lovely commemorative plate.

Although I retired from Boots in 1988 at the age of sixty five, I have never been short of things to do. Fortnightly visits to the Probus club give me contact with a group of people who I have known for many years. I still work in my garden which keeps me as active as I can be and spend as much time as I can with my growing family. The garden has always been a focus for family get-togethers when the weather would allow. Each year I would grow an array of colourful flowers which provided cut flowers for many months and I must have given away two hundred bunches or so each year.

When Nan died in 1991, it left a great void in my life. She had been my constant companion for forty eight years and it had been Nan's hope to be able to celebrate our golden wedding anniversary together, but it was not to be. I was devastated of course, but with the help of my family and friends, I slowly began to learn to live alone. Clive asked me to do some jobs at his school in Norden. I drove the minibus, taking senior citizens three times a week to and from the Norden School Luncheon Club. Sometimes, I took the children to different venues on the bus. This continued for twenty years, until I became the eldest senior citizen on the bus! As a keen gardener, Clive also knew that I would be willing to help look after the school greenhouse and gardens with the help of the children and show them how to grow plants from seeds and cuttings. I continued doing this until I was no longer able to cut the large bushes and plant the tubs. More importantly, this work gave me another lease on life and a focus for my time. Clive also began to take me with him as he refereed football matches throughout Lancashire and Cumbria each Saturday of the football season and occasionally we went to a few Yorkshire teams. I am still enjoying watching him and when we visit the West Lancashire Football teams, I am well looked after.

I am very proud of what Clive has achieved at Norden. They always represent Rochdale schools at sport within Greater Manchester and his gymnasts are always in the top six in the country. One year his summer soccer school was the biggest in Europe and in 2013 Norden was the top Sports school in England.

Eileen Morley

In 1994, the professional organist at the Church left and Eileen Morley, a member of the choir for many years was asked to take over. Eileen had a lovely alto voice and was an excellent pianist so an ideal candidate for the job. It took her a couple of months to change from pianist to organist but she became very proficient.

Eileen was the niece of my friends Stanley Jackson and Hilda Hanson who were brother and sister. She had been divorced for ten years, was seventeen years younger than I and had three grown up children. We had a coach trip from the church to York and I was sitting near the front with Stanley and Doreen and Eileen was sitting at the back with two of her friends, a mother and daughter. As we left the coach at York, I noticed that Eileen's two friends had left her and she was alone. I asked her if she would like to join us and I saw how happy she looked when she accepted the invitation. It was to be the start of a lovely friendship, and eventually we became constant companions, each of us still having our own homes.

In 2002, I was four days from death from colon cancer, with a poor prognosis, but after my operation, Eileen, together with my family looked after me and I recovered. Sadly, early in 2004 she got breast cancer and eventually died on 11th January 2005. She was only sixty three years of age. Her grave in Heywood Cemetery, which when possible I visit, has a lovely view of St Luke's Church which she had attended all her life. After her funeral her three children, who had never contributed to the upkeep of Eileen's home decided that I was no longer part of their family and I don't see them with the exception of Amanda who was married to and now divorced from her youngest son. They had two children, Robert and Olivia, who sometimes come to visit me. Robert was only a year old when Eileen died.

Nan, in her conversations with the Inner Wheel friends once said, "One fellow is enough for me, but I think that if I died first, Jack might find another wife." I did find a companion, but my marriage of forty eight years to Nan, would last me for ever.

On the 13th July 2007, together with the M.P. James Dobbin I reopened the Police Station which had been closed for several years. One and a half a million pounds had been spent on converting the interior of the building into offices, whilst retaining many of the original features such as two cell doors, the Court Room and the beautiful staircase. It is now known as T.O.P.S. (The Old Police Station) Thirteen of my policemen were also present along with two of the magistrates. It was a very pleasant ceremony. Since then, I have been invited back as a guest of the manager who said that they have 'adopted' me! After a short speech I was presented with a framed photo of the premises as they were when I left in 1974.

Reflections

Family

The birth of our three children Ray, Clive and Lynne were all joyous events. Ray was born on the third of March 1946 approximately nine months after a lovely week's holiday in Llandudno which Nan and I had whilst I was in the Navy. She always said it was her favourite holiday resort in the UK! Clive was definitely a product of Switzerland being born on the twenty third of January 1950, but Lynne, who was born on the second of October 1950 was definitely home-grown.

When it was their turn to get married, we were delighted at their choices; firstly Barbara Heap who married Ray, then Anne Booth who married Clive and lastly John Coxell who married Lynne. This resulted in the love of six grandchildren; Nicholas and Janine, Andrea and Lyndsey, and Jonathan and Benjamin. Sadly, Nan died before any of our grandchildren got married. Six lovely weddings took place without the presence of that wonderful lady… she would have been so proud.

Nature took its course and by 2014, I had eleven great grandchildren who give me tremendous joy. It is lovely to hear the affection with which the family talk about their mother and grandmother as they reflect on the many happy memories they have. People who know about Nan's calmness and have experienced my quick temper have asked if we ever fell out over the forty eight years we were married. I tell them, "No it's impossible to fall out with someone who doesn't answer back!"

Father Christmas

In my early years, Father Christmas always managed to get to 11 West View and I was very fond of him, but it wasn't until Christmas Day of the last two years of my mother's life in 1993 and 1994; whilst visiting the Home in Low Moor, Clitheroe where she and other very elderly people resided; that I really became acquainted with him.

Stephen Jaquest, who lived as an orphan with my family from 1946 was regarded by me as a step brother. In 1992, whilst still living at 13 Wilson St Clitheroe, and looking after my mother, he had a severe heart attack and died. I was on holiday in North Wales with the Jacksons and went straight back to Clitheroe to help sort out the mess my mother, who was aged 96, was now in. It was a case of getting her into a nursing home quickly and Cecil and I were able to accommodate her in a very nice home which had once been St Paul's Church Vicarage in Low Moor. It was owned by an ex-Blackburn Rover's footballer and his wife, a hospital sister. That first year, they asked if I would be Father Christmas for the thirty odd elderly residents, which I did for three years until mother at the age of 99, died peacefully at the Nursing Home. This was the start of twenty years of helping Father Christmas with the mammoth task of meeting many young boys and girls to listen to their Christmas wishes, firstly at Norden Primary School, then at St Catherine's and for the last eight years, at St Edwards School.

There is tremendous pleasure to be found in seeing the happiness of thousands of small children, their eyes glittering as they tell you what they want and expect on Christmas Day. Christmas Carols, albeit mostly the same, were sung with such gusto with the help of the teachers. Nationality never seemed to matter and each year seemed better and better. I'm sure Father Christmas smiled a lot beneath his beard!

Numerous times, tiny little girls would say that they wanted a baby (of course a baby brother or sister). A little girl once said that she wanted a horse. "A rocking horse?" asked Father Christmas. "No, a real horse" came the reply, her mother nodding, to confirm the child's request.

Many children would ask where the reindeer were and so it was a godsend when St Edwards got their two donkeys and the reindeer were able to have a rest in their stable. A special photo shows Santa with the donkeys. I wonder if Father Christmas ever retires?

The Blackbird

Like millions of people, whilst gardening I often experienced the company of the birds. Some would come quite close, especially blackbirds and robins and in 2008, I was joined by a beautiful young female blackbird which for six years seemed to have spent most of its life in my front garden in the trees and bushes. It wasn't very interested in the bird table or the feeding containers, but enjoyed the small bird bath. Its favourite food was dried porridge oats, which it wanted on the flagstones in front of my back door. The five foot iron railings of the sports field a metre away became its perch. Sometimes I would sit on the step and it pecked away at the food at my feet, but it never came on my hand. It had a mate, but the mate never came close. The pair nested about eighty yards away, across the sports field in a garden in Westwood Avenue. Between 2009 and 2014, they had thirteen offspring which all arrived for feeding. Last year (2013) she had four and one day she fed all four, two at my feet and the other two sitting on the railings opposite the back door. She wasn't half busy!

I talked to it but probably the only words it understood were 'Good girl'. It did however, fly across the field to me when I whistled, and would alight on the railings. If I didn't know it was around, it used to make a peculiar clucking noise which indicated that it wanted feeding. Twice recently, in June 2014, it came into my hallway through the open front door and once into my kitchen.

On the 2nd of July, it was missing, but yesterday, the 4th of July at 7pm it was standing near my back door and I realised that it was dying of old age. It went to the bird bath and had a drink. I wanted to get it into the Holly tree a few yards away, to prevent cats which frequently come through my garden from getting it, but it actually flew into the lower branches of the tree.

During the early morning it must have managed to get back for a drink as at 7am, I found it dead at the side of the bath. I am going to miss that special little bird and the joy of listening to it chirping and singing. It was today buried underneath the trees in my front garden where it spent most of its life, not far away from the spot where forty years ago I buried Shane, my boxer dog.

War medals

My years in the Royal Navy are still very vivid and each day at sea was a case of survival, no matter whether in the Atlantic Ocean, the Bay of Biscay or the Arctic seas. The Russians first issued a commemorative medal in 1985 to all sailors who had been on the Russian Convoys; forty years after the war in Europe had ended. I wasn't aware of this medal until in 1992 I was endeavouring to trace friends of Stephen Jaquest at Edgeworth Orphanage. It had been their annual reunion day and I met an ex-sailor who knew him well during their time in this isolated home on Haslingden Moors. It turned out that both he and I had been on the convoys and so he asked me whether or not I had received the Russian Medal. As I had not been awarded this honour, he told me how to apply for it and so I did. I received a letter back from the Ministry of Defence to say that the Russians had not made enough of these medals but that a second lot was to be struck and so in 1992 I received the 40th Anniversary Medal from the Russians.

It was many years later that the Queen decided that this medal could be worn along with our own medals. The British Government had considered the Atlantic Star medal sufficient, but so much pressure was put on them, particularly by the Daily Mail, that in about 2010 an Arctic Star lapel badge was issued to all surviving Arctic Convoy veterans and then after some pressure from Russia, the

Artic Star medal was finally struck.

The Arctic Star medal was given firstly in 2013 to the survivors of the Russian Convoys, approximately three hundred of them, then posthumously to each family who had lost someone who had died whilst in the Arctic waters. I was handed mine at St Edwards School, Castleton; where Lynne was the headmistress; by Bishop Mark the Bishop of Middleton, at a special school assembly. Both local newspapers, The Heywood Advertiser and Clitheroe Advertiser made quite a fuss over the medal.

On October 13th 2014, I was also presented with another war medal: The Ushakov medal which was presented to both Royal Navy veterans and Merchant Seamen who had served their country during the second world war on the Arctic convoys. I went along with my daughter Lynne, her husband John and my daughter-in-law Anne, to Manchester Town Hall. We had coffee on arrival and then went into the Great Hall where the ceremony was to take part. In all, there were about seventy veterans who received the Ushakov medal that day from the Russian Ambassador, A. Yakovenko.

In his speech he said; "It is a huge privilege for me to thank you on behalf of the Russian Government for the invaluable contribution you and your comrades-in-arms made to the defeat of Nazi Germany. What you did seventy years ago, taking part in what Sir Winston Churchill rightly called *the worst journey in the world,* was extraordinary even among what is considered to be beyond the call of duty. Thousands of Allied seamen lost their lives as the British ships sailed in the unwelcoming, stormy seas of the Arctic Ocean under a constant threat of being attacked by German U-boats and aircraft. Your heroism will always be remembered in Russia and Britain. Your deeds will continue to serve as the supreme expression of bravery and a high point in human spirit.

I am confident that it was not by accident that our nations found themselves on the right side of history, which the followers of ideology of hatred wanted to stop, while depriving nations of their unalienable right to decide their destiny. The allied effort required all the best in the national spirit of the British and the peoples of the Soviet Union, the very strength of character that we are rightfully proud of. The comradeship-in-arms, which was born at the truly juncture of history will forever remain an important part of European spiritual heritage and our bilateral relationship, including the ties between the two navies."

After speeches were made, we were presented with the medal which I know was a proud moment for everyone. Our photos were taken and a lot of interest was shown in the stories we all had to tell. Once the ceremony was over, we were served afternoon tea where we all had chance to chat and hear the stories others had to tell. It was a wonderful day.

Life with Jack and Nan : Family reflections

As a father....

Sport has always played a prominent place in Jack's leisure time and his love of football and cricket was passed on to his sons.

Ray's first memory of being a Blackburn Rover's fan was when his dad took him to Ewood Park for a game with Tottenham Hotspur. The ground was that full that he was passed overhead from the back to the front and ended up watching the game sitting on the grass with a lot of other children. His own love of cricket started when he went to matches, being the scorer with his Dad who was the batsman for the Lancashire Police, and also watching him play for Rawtenstall.

Clive too remembers watching his dad play cricket for Rawtenstall and opening the batting when he played against some of the finest West Indian players who ever played. Recollections of watching his dad playing cricket against Lancashire and against England cricketers are also proud memories for him.

Social events and holidays have always evoked happy memories and all the family have their own specific memories. Bank holidays were something for the family to really look forward to when they would go on walks to places like Bolton Abbey, the Ribble Valley, the Yorkshire Dales and sometimes as far afield as Wales. Ray remembers these outings fondly especially when he went with his Dad and Mum, Barbara, Nick and Janine, and sometimes with Lynne and John; the day sometimes ending up with a picnic or a pub meal. The early memories when Nick would lag behind and they would have to stop to let him catch up, then set off again as soon as he did, were hilarious and still make Ray and Barbara smile. Those times without Mum are sorely missed.

Holidays when his mum and dad, together with Lynne and John and the boys, joined Ray and Barbara in Ballston Lake in the USA are memories that Ray and Barbara will always treasure. They would go swimming in Lake George and Lake Lucerne and visit Niagra Falls and Albany. Many happy times were also had together at Ray and Barbara's own swimming pool at Eastwood Drive. Ray says that he and Barbara would specifically like to thank Dad and Mum for the love and hospitality they gave when they returned from the USA and stayed with them until finding their own home in Holcombe Brook in 1984.

As a child, Clive remembers his dad having to carry him on his shoulders up Pendle Hill as he was either too tired or too lazy to walk on his own. Another fond memory which Clive has is of the family packing tightly into the Simca and travelling with five lots of luggage down to Dover, across France and into Switzerland for their annual summer holiday. Games were often invented by Jack and Nan to keep the children occupied for the long journey ahead.

Lynne recalls her wonderful childhood which has given her many special memories of time spent with her mum and dad and two brothers.

"Dad always figured strongly in my childhood

memories. From an early age I can remember him telling me about nature and how important it was. We always went on daily walks either when he had a day off from the police or when he returned from work. The walks always had a nature lesson to them and I can remember at the age of five being able to recall the names of many wild flowers and wild animals. Our family always had animals and one day when I was four our dog Prince brought home a mole which he had caught in the fields opposite our house. Dad let me touch it and feel its soft fur even though it was dead. From that moment, my love of animals and nature started, which he always encouraged.

When I was eight, we had just moved to Heywood and I had just started at my third primary school when a lunchtime supervisor told me that her dog had had puppies and that I could have one if I wanted one. I felt confident that it wouldn't be a problem so after school, without telling my parents, I went to her house and then carried an eight week old puppy home under my school jumper. I arrived home with a Boxer crossed with a Labrador, so not even a small puppy! Mum I don't think, was overly impressed with this idea of mine but I was certain dad would let me keep him. Dad arrived home, and yes we did keep him. Dad called him Shane and the dog really became his and he was soon followed by a stray dog from the police station, a rough collie called Laddie.

Dad was a keen sportsman and I can remember the weekends in the summer months were spent travelling round Lancashire to various cricket grounds, which I always enjoyed. Dad always took me to watch the cricket and play with the other children whilst mum made the teas for the cricket team with the other wives. He always encouraged my brothers and I to take part in sports which we all did and continue to do.

As a teenager dad and I had one thing which just the two of us did together and that was to watch the latest James Bond films as soon as they came out at the Odeon in Bury. Dad knew the manager and so I used to get special treats.

Our holidays in Switzerland, together as a family, were always very special. Dad did all the driving even though it took two days to get there. It always used to make me laugh that dad had to have a shave in the morning before we drove any further on the journey, so out would come the shaving soap and brush and the flask of cold water (Standards had to be maintained !). We had lots of fun and laughter in our childhood and this continued when mum and dad looked after my sons Jonathan and Ben.

There is nothing better than a happy childhood and spending time with a very special dad!"

As a grandad and a great-grandad...

Jack is loved and respected by all of his grandchildren and his ever growing collection of great-grandchildren. He is the undisputed head of the family! Once again, the most prominent memories are of family occasions. These memories which Andrea and Lyndsey recall express those feelings...

'As children, grandad was like a 'gentle giant'; a figure that towered above us but one who never made us feel scared. He was, and still is, as stubborn as an ox, but he has a heart of gold! We spent many Saturday nights at grandma and grandad's house. Grandma would be playing cards with her friends whilst we snuggled on the sofa with grandad watching Tripods, Dallas and Dynasty. We always looked forward to our supper of ham and chips; not very healthy, but very enjoyable.

On a Sunday morning we would get in bed with grandad whilst he told us many different versions of 'The Fishy Story'. He would take our imaginations on the journeys of a little fish who got lost in a stream and all about his adventures along the way. We never got bored of this story.

We spent many hours with grandad when we travelled

for twenty four hours in a car to Switzerland. We preferred to travel with grandad and grandma because they had the best sweets.

Bonfire night is full of memories of grandad organising big fires, and eating black peas made grandma's Swiss way. We were always so proud of our grandparents because it felt like they were so well respected by the community.

Every Boxing Day would be comprised of a big meal at their house with the whole family and the icing on the cake would be a big bin liner full of Boots goodies. We all got one and it felt like Christmas Day all over again.

As grown-ups, we have been fortunate to have been able to spend a lot of time with grandad, listening to all his amazing stories whilst we shop together. We often talk about grandma and remember our times together, but he also gives us the gift of his memories of grandma and their life together, about how they met and fell in love. Grandma was a massive part of our lives but was taken from us far too soon.

Grandad has tried his best to impart his thriftiness onto us, but somehow it hasn't worked. Grandad loves a bargain… half price, buy one get one free, but despite his money saving disposition, he is the most generous person we know. He gives his love to us all so compassionately and is very proud of everything we achieve, as long of course as it doesn't involve getting a tattoo! Grandad really is special to us. He is the 'Godfather' of our family and we are blessed to have him as our grandad.'

Many of these memories are echoed by Nick and Janine. They too remember snuggling up in grandma and grandad's bed when they both went to stay at their house every other weekend. The story of the little fish played a part in these visits too and Janine remembers Shane the dog also nestled at the bottom of the bed. Nick has memories of grandad collecting both him and Janine from school sometimes, and once, much to the envy of Nick's classmates, his grandad arrived in a Police car! Mint

Imperials were always to hand, and occasionally they would stop off at the Police Station in Whitefield. Nick even remembers his grandad putting him a cell once... Nick says, 'those Friday nights would be spent in front of the telly watching programmes that were not normally allowed at home.' As well as telling the story of the little fish, Nick says that one of grandad's jobs on Saturday mornings was to do the hoovering which he thinks was quite progressive for the early 1970's! Nicks recalls that usually Saturday afternoons involved football, (as it still does), during which time grandma would cook tea for the whole family. 'I'm still not sure how they managed to fit all of us in the conservatory,' he says.

Bank holiday walks also feature in their recollections, especially the trips to Bolton Abbey where they would all have a picnic and try to cross the river. Nick remembers going to Clitheroe to visit Great Gran and during the car journey at Christmas, they would count Christmas trees and at other times they would count 'For Sale' signs.

When Janine and her family left for America, leaving grandad and grandma behind was difficult and even though they visited, she remembers missing her grandparents. This made their return a few years later all the more special as they went to live at Jesmond Dene until they had bought a new home. She says that grandad managed to cope with them in his usual calm and authoritative manner, and this included their dog Storm who was a rather crazy animal! In Janine's words: 'He is still looking after us even now; coming into work for his dental check-ups and bringing flowers with him from his wonderful garden in the summer. Everyone at the surgery comments on how lovely, friendly and smartly dressed he is and he always brightens up our day. The huge presence he had as a policeman and security guard is still with him, and always will be.'

Ben says that his most prominent memory is of the time when he dragged his grandad through the conveniently loosened bars in his fence in order to play cricket on the school playing field! They couldn't just play cricket on the field, as that 'just wasn't cricket', but had to walk half way across the school field to the artificial wicket; six stumps in hand, as well as a cricket bat and ball and then set up to play.

Ben recalls, 'I would always bat and ask him to repeatedly bowl ball after ball. Looking back on it, a few things come to mind. The first being that this was a seventy year old man climbing through fences in order to play cricket with his grandson and secondly, what was it that turned me into a bowler and not a batsman? We still talk about cricket now every time I see him and he still likes to hear how I do every week; probably to see if I put into practice what he showed me all those years ago. '

Jonathan's memories of being at his grandma and grandad's house when they were children are of asking for really odd things for supper – the sort of things their mum and dad would never have let them have, had they known. He remembers asking for a large chunk of cucumber on more than one occasion and a tin of sweetcorn. "Quite often we would have pancakes for breakfast" says Jonathan, "but not the normal type, Grandma and Grandad always had a box of American style pancake powder. They made the best pancakes."

Swiss holidays also feature in Jonathan's memories: "I remember our trips to Switzerland with them both – always a great holiday but not much to do in the car for two days. It took two days because we always went down the French B roads to avoid the motorways. As a child I loved it. We would eventually find a 'Frites' van on the side of the road for lunch. Grandad would always have a metal tin of a mixture of sweets and mints in the glove-box of his car; it never seemed to get emptier even though Ben and I always raided the box every time we got in the car."

As the author of this book, it has been my pleasure to work with Jack, a man who has worked tirelessly all his life for his family. During the last forty years it has been my privilege to be a member of this family and his support and love during good times and bad have made this time very special. In the early 1970's as a new member of the family I was always made to feel a complete part of this wonderful dynasty and I too have many happy memories of holidays, Christmases, weddings, christenings and outings. We have laughed together, given and taken advice, cried at the sad and difficult times, but Jack's love for his family has always shone through. It is more recently though, that I have come to know him really well as we sat for hours talking about his experiences and taking the many photos which might just represent a brief moment in his life. On one such trip we went to visit the gate where he gave Nan her first kiss and true to form, he was able to take me straight there even after more than sixty years. As he stood in front of that gate looking out over the field where he had walked with his future bride, the poignancy of the moment was not lost on me. Jack has been a sailor, a policeman, a husband, a father, a grandfather and a great grandfather; but most of all in his heart, he has been, and still is a wonderful family man.

About the Author

Anne Booth is the daughter-in-law of Jack Wilson and lives in Rochdale. She has previously published two novels, both fiction: A Tragedy Too Far, and The Joiner's Secret; but this is her first experience of writing a biography. Her passion is genealogy as well as social history and this biography embraces both. When Jack was encouraged by his family to write down some of his 'little stories', he approached Anne to help him. About a year and a half later, this biography is the outcome of that joint venture.

HMS Cooke

Jack and his Navy pals

View of Loch Ewe 2014

Memorial to the sailors who sailed the Arctic from
Loch Ewe to Russia in WW2

Clitheroe Cenotaph

Clitheroe Police Station 2014

Blackpool August 1944

Numbers 9 &11 West View, Clitheroe

St James School, Clitheroe 2014

Heywood Police Station 2014

Inspector Wilson 1964

Vic Swinney and Satan

Cricket 1968

Family gathering 1970's - Rotary 'do'

Presentation of the Ushakov Medal 13th October 2014

Lightning Source UK Ltd.
Milton Keynes UK
UKOW06f1503050315

247344UK00011B/66/P